LEADER'S GUIDE

Petersburg, Kentucky, USA

Demolishing Strongholds Leader's Guide

Second printing February 2008

For more information, write:
Answers in Genesis
2800 Bullittsburg Church Rd
Petersburg, KY 41080

ISBN: 1-60092-030-6

Based on video presentations from the
Demolishing Strongholds Conference
Higher Ground Conference Center
West Harrison, Indiana
March 17-19, 2006

Written and compiled by Holly Varnum

Interior layout by Diane King
Cover design by Brandie Lucas
Edited by Gary Vaterlaus

Printed in the United States of America

TABLE OF CONTENTS

MISSION STATEMENT

The mission of the Demolishing Strongholds curriculum is to educate and equip teenagers with the tools necessary to embrace the biblical worldview, identify the foundation of secular worldviews, stand firm on the authority of Scripture "from the very first verse," and to use this knowledge to reach the lost for Christ.

INTRODUCTION

Getting today's youth to take a stand for Christ seems much more difficult in the present than in times past; in fact, young people today appear to be taken in by the influences of a godless culture with alarming regularity. The lines between the sacred and secular have become more "fuzzy" and indistinguishable as churches try to engage their culture by inadvertently becoming more like it.

Statistics show that a significant number of Christian young people are less grounded and more uncommitted in their faith than their adult counterparts would expect. According to David Kinnaman of The Barna Group in his research report entitled, "Ministry to Mosaics: Teens and the Supernatural" (January 2006), "Teenagers are members of the Mosaic generation, those Americans currently age three to 21. The term 'Mosaic' is a great way to describe teens' patchwork of values and lifestyles: they are the ultimate collage artists, pulling ideas and input from a variety of sources that consist of great diversity of flavors." In the area of church attendance, Mosaics are least likely to attend church in a typical weekend (33%), and only 27% of Mosaics say they are absolutely committed to the Christian faith.

What's a youth leader to do to make a difference for Christ and to ignite a desire in today's teens to totally surrender their hearts and minds to the Lord (Romans 12:1–2)? The first prerequisite in answering this question is to understand the underlying problem that has caused the downward spiral of decreasing Christian commitment. *Demolishing Strongholds* sets out to present the foundational issues that permeate our culture and serve to weaken the Church. We have been bombarded by anti-God philosophies that have caused our faith to waver because we are not equipped to respond to the attack. Throughout this course, teacher and students alike will be given information, practical advice, and scriptural backing to know why the Bible is the absolute authoritative Word of God, to understand the "war" we are engaged in, and to be able to counteract the stronghold the world system desires to have on us.

As a ministry, *Answers in Genesis* has taken on the challenge of training others to defend their faith in order to:

- proclaim the gospel of Jesus Christ effectively,
- answer questions surrounding the book of Genesis, as it is one of the most-attacked books of the Bible,
- develop a biblical worldview, and
- expose the bankruptcy of evolutionary ideas.

During the course of this study, students will be shown that "facts" don't speak for themselves, but must be interpreted. That is, there aren't separate sets of "evidences" for evolution and creation—we all deal with the same evidence (we all live on the same earth, have the same fossils, observe the same animals, etc.). The difference lies in how we interpret what we study. The Bible—the history book of the universe—provides a reliable, eyewitness account of the beginning of all things, and can be trusted to tell the truth in all areas it touches on. Therefore, we are able to use it to help us make sense of this present world. When properly understood, the evidence confirms the biblical account.

HOW TO USE THIS CURRICULUM

Please note that the material from the student workbook is included within this Leader's Guide as it appears in a lesson. What you as the leader should do and say is presented at the beginning of each lesson and in the margins next to the images of the student pages. You also have the blanks and answers filled in so that you can discuss them with your students.

Session Requirements

For each lesson, you will need:

- DVD player, projector, screen (if not using your computer to play the DVDs), TV monitor (if group is of a smaller size)
- Leader's Guide
- Bible
- The appropriate number of student workbooks (one per student)
- CD-Rom with supplementary materials
- Data projector for showing PowerPoint slides. Alternatively, you could copy the PowerPoint slides onto transparency slides and use an overhead projector.

Other recommended materials:

- *Strong's Exhaustive Concordance of the Bible*
- It is recommended that the instructor view AiG's DVD entitled "A God of Suffering?" prior to Lesson 4.

Participant's Requirements

For each lesson, the participant will need:

- Student Workbook
- Bible
- Writing utensil

PLANNING AHEAD

Several of the lessons require advance planning (more than a week) for certain aspects of the lesson. These are listed below:

For Lesson 3

Note for the Object Lesson: If you have access to a computer with internet and can project it onto a screen, log on to www.youthonline.ca/games/difference/ and choose one of the items for your youth to compare. It's much harder than it looks. The first illustration is the "real thing" while the second has several subtle variations on it.

For Lesson 5

1. Recruit three adult "guests" that your youth group is not familiar with to set up a version of the 50s–70s show "To Tell the Truth." Choose the occupation of one of the adults as the career to be highlighted. Ask that individual if he/she will write a short, first-person paragraph about his/her job that you can read to the group before questioning begins. Tell all three of the volunteers that they will be questioned by the youth panel about that occupation and need to try to sound convincing with their answers.
2. Also, find a show tune to play (you may be able to purchase a download of the "To Tell the Truth" theme song for a nominal fee) for the entrance and exit of the contestants.
3. Choose three youth group members to be the "judges." Tell them ahead of time what the game involves and what the occupation

will be that they will be questioning. Ask each of them to prepare several questions they could ask the contestants.

4. The day of the contest, have them come to youth group a little early so that you can go over the game procedures with them. (See Lesson 5 for details.)

For Lesson 7

Materials:

- Several items of different ages, with some things looking older that really aren't (Begin collecting these early on so that you will have a good sized collection of 5–10 items. Newer items with scratches or rust will give the appearance of age.)
- A table to display them on
- Pieces of tape or stickers with numbers to identify each item
- 3x5 cards for the students to write the numbers in order from youngest to oldest

Note: Between Lessons 7 & 8, the Optional Activity is a museum tour to compare dates given to the different displays. Try to make plans to go as a group (include only those who are serious about this assignment) as a "field trip." Those who participate should be prepared to report back to the group at the beginning of Lesson 8.

For Lesson 8

An example of how scientists are misguided by their presuppositions is included on the following website: www.bbc.co.uk/sn/prehisoric_life/games/fakes_mistakes/. Intended to be a quiz to point out scientific hoaxes, this activity shows how faulty dating methods and reasoning can illustrate hoaxes of scientific claims of "accurate" information. It would be an extremely effective object lesson for your students.

In order to use it with a large group, you would need to be able to project the site from a computer to a screen or white wall. If you do not have access to such equipment but have a computer (with internet access) and a printer, you can print the slides from this quiz onto transparencies. Another option would be to print them out on paper and have the teens work in groups to answer one or more questions.

For Lesson 9

Materials:

- A hair dryer and a styling brush
- One or two cans of hair spray
- Camera for "Before" and "After" photos
- Brightly-colored gawdy clothing
- A megaphone or other voice-carrying device
- Three small rooms or areas where the different acts can prepare
- A bag or more of Smarties™

Recruit 4–5 teens ahead of time to perform the following tasks:

1. Two or three teens – one to get his/her hair "done" in as crazy a way as possible using hair spray and a hair dryer, the other one or two to be the stylist(s)
2. One teen to dress in the outlandish clothing
3. One teen to use the megaphone to talk loudly to the crowd

For Lesson 10

Materials:

- Fine sand (available in hobby stores)
- Squirt guns (preferably enough for each student to use one – these are usually available at dollar stores, Wal-Mart, or Target.)
- Water source to fill the squirt guns prior to the meeting
- A small unbreakable bowl
- A pan in which to place the sand and bowl

LESSON COMPONENTS

We provide a lesson overview (also included in the Student Workbook at the beginning of each student lesson) and lesson objectives for the leader at the beginning of each lesson.

Each lesson should take approximately 50–60 minutes to complete and is divided into the following components:

1. **Laying the Groundwork** (5–10 minutes)

   During this time, welcome the participants to the session, make any announcements, begin with prayer, etc.

   Spend five minutes reviewing the homework from the previous week. Encourage participants to share what they've learned and to hold each other accountable for what they're learning. (You, the leader, need to decide what this would look like with your group.) Also, make sure you have the group read/recite the memory passage out loud each week. In addition to independent memorization as part of their homework, the group repetition will enable them to learn this passage even more solidly.

   Go right into the ***Object Lesson/Icebreaker*** for the lesson. The power of an object lesson is in its simplicity. Resist the temptation to explain all the deep symbolism you've been able to uncover. One of the quickest ways to ruin an object lesson is to try to make it more than it is. Make just one truth visible to your students—that's enough. Prepare the best object lesson you can, but keep it simple, and remember that it's the Holy Spirit—not your object lesson—that instructs and changes students.

2. **View the DVD** (20–25 minutes)

   During this segment of each lesson, the students have been given key thoughts/ideas to complete in their workbooks. While you are previewing the session, make notes about specific areas that you are aware of that may be an issue for your students. Feel free to take a few minutes following this part of the lesson to get them to open up and discuss these issues.

3. **Get Into the Word** (15–20 minutes)

   The goal of this lesson component is to show students the relevance of God's Word in daily life, school, and work situations. In the course of the first three lessons, students will be guided to a deeper meaning of the passage(s) used through word study or questions related to application of the verses. At the end of Lesson 3, you will come to a section entitled, "Developing a Biblical Worldview through Inductive Bible Study." From this point on in the curriculum, the students will be guided through the components of Inductive Bible Study to help them learn an effective way to delve meaningfully into God's Word. Many of the student resources for the Bible study may be found on the CD-Rom. By the end of this course, the students should have enough experience and practice with this Bible study method to utilize it personally on a daily basis.

   For Lessons 4–7 students will use the handout, "Original Greek of Key Words" found on the CD-Rom in Lesson 4. This will help them to complete their inductive study of the Bible passages for these weeks.

   Another aspect of *Get into the Word* will include Scripture memory. A few minutes during this part of each lesson should be devoted to reading/reciting and reviewing the Scripture passage (2 Timothy 4:1–8). Many of the introduction sections of the lessons are focused on helping the students analyze and really understand the passage content.

4. **Find the Focus** (5 minutes)

   Application of knowledge should be the object of any lesson, especially when it comes to learning and living out the Scriptures. The final few minutes of each lesson should be devoted to helping your students meditate upon what they have taken in with each lesson and write down how that information has and will continue to make a difference in their lives. Feel free to take extra time for this part of the lesson to really get your students to take something away with them from the lesson.

   Additionally, this Leader's Guide will provide supplementary ideas for extension activities the students can do to further reinforce the thrust of each lesson. Any worksheets for such ideas will be provided in an electronic format on the supplementary CD-Rom.

5. **Homework** (1–2 minutes)

   This section is designed to encourage participants to continue to evaluate and apply the content of the lesson during the following week. A minute or two at the end of class time to clarify the assignment is allotted.

   At the end of most lessons you will hand out a page or more of valuable information for reading homework. These articles are designed to build any Christian's toolbox with information to help him or her deal with nonbiblical worldviews/beliefs. These are found on the CD-Rom and should be printed out and distributed during the *Homework* time. Though certainly not exhaustive, these handouts provide an initial foundation for a biblical worldview in relation to some of the most common topics that a teenager might encounter when defending his or her faith.

Optional Activities

Many teenagers in your group may desire to dig deeper into the content of this curriculum. For several of the lessons, optional activities have been included. All *Optional Activities* will be referenced in the Leader's Guide and are included on the CD-Rom for duplication.

For those students who take the time to do this, you may want to have them come to the meeting/class 15–20 minutes early to discuss what they gleaned from their study. Having a separate time with them will encourage their faith and may spur others to want to put forth the effort.

Some youth groups have additional requirements for students who are preparing for a missions trip or who are trying to earn camp scholarships, so you may want to use these activities for such a purpose.

How to get the most out of this curriculum

1. Be flexible as you facilitate the group discussion. We have provided suggested responses; however, allow participants to discuss their views, within reason, while guiding them to understand what the Bible teaches.

2. Take your time as you go through the questions—feel free to spend more time on some sections/questions than others. Allow the participants' interest level to guide the discussion.

3. Do not allow any one person to monopolize the discussion—be careful to include all participants.

4. *Consider spending two sessions on each lesson to get the full benefit of spending adequate time on the content of each lesson.* Though set up for 13 sessions, this curriculum could easily be expanded to cover 26 sessions.

For more Information

There are many excellent resources that can encourage teenagers in their walk with the Lord and equip them to defend their faith in a hostile environment. Some suggested resources are listed here.

The New Answers Book, Ken Ham, General Editor, Master Books, 2006.

Pocket Guide for Effective Evangelism, Ken Ham, Answers in Genesis, 2006.

Nothing But the Truth, Brian Edwards, Evangelical Press, 2006.

Evolution Exposed, Roger Patterson, Answers in Genesis, 2006.

War of the Worldviews, Ken Ham et al., Answers in Genesis, 2005.

Always Ready, Greg Bahnsen, Covenant Media Press, 1996.

Questions booklet series, Answers in Genesis

These resources are available from AnswersBookstore.com or by calling Answers in Genesis at 1-800-778-3390.

About the Demolishing Strongholds Curriculum

In an effort to target the needs of young people and prepare them for encountering the secular world after high school, the concept for the *Demolishing Strongholds* Conference was born. Following the successful conference in the Spring of 2006, Answers in Genesis decided to make this important teaching available to youth all over the world.

It is with a deep care and concern for the teenage population that this project has come to fruition. Presented in a visually appealing and forthright manner, *Demolishing Strongholds* strives to maintain high interest and deep teaching in such a way that your youth population will desire to impact their culture for Christ.

Acknowledgements

We would like to thank the youth pastors who helped us in field testing and evaluating this curriculum. Your suggestions were most helpful.

WAR OF THE WORLDVIEWS PART 1

CAN WE REALLY TRUST THE BIBLE?

OVERVIEW

When speaking at a church or conference for the first time, Ken Ham will often begin his talk with asking questions of the audience members to get them to see how America has become "less Christian" than it once was. He then makes the following statement:

> "I believe the main reason the church is not 'touching' the culture like it used to, is because, by and large, the culture has 'touched' the church. Most of the church has allowed the authority of the Word of God to be undermined beginning in Genesis by compromising with evolutionary ideas and/or millions of years. After years of such compromise, the foundational basis of the culture, the absolute authority of the Word of God, has been replaced with a different foundation – one that makes fallible man the ultimate authority. As a result of this foundational change, which the Church itself helped to bring about, the culture has changed in structure from a Christian one to an increasingly secular one."

The thrust of this first lesson, presented by Ken Ham, is to establish the authority of the Scriptures and to get students to understand that there is a culture war stemming from two distinct worldviews—creation (biblical) and evolution (atheistic/humanistic/secular).

OBJECTIVES

As a result of this lesson, students will be able to:

1. Explain some of the historical, archeological, and literary evidence for the authority of the Scriptures.
2. Identify two distinct worldviews—stemming from creation and evolution standpoints.
3. Demonstrate foundational knowledge that supports the biblical creation account (DNA, fossils, human genome/one race, animals/kinds).
4. Define science, faith, and religion.
5. Communicate the difference between observational science and historical science.

BEFORE THE LESSON

Opening Prayer, Announcements, etc.

Object Lesson: Trusting God's Word, Our Spiritual Compass

Theme: The Bible is our spiritual compass.

Materials needed: A compass

Scriptures:

> Your word is a lamp to my feet, and a light to my path (Psalm 119:105).
>
> Jesus said to him, "I am the way, the truth, and the life. No one comes to the Father except through Me (John 14:6).

DEMOLISHING STRONGHOLDS

I am sure that probably all of you have seen a compass. A compass is used to find the right direction to get you to where you want to go. The compass has four main directions. They are North, South, East, and West. The needle of the compass always points North. If the needle is pointing in that direction (point to the North) and I want to go South, I would go that direction (point in the opposite direction from what the needle is pointing.) With the needle pointing North, if I wanted to go East, I would go in that direction (point to the East.) If the needle sometimes pointed North and at other times it pointed to the South, East, or West, I would never be able to use the compass to find my way. I would wander around, hopelessly lost. ***The compass must always point in the right direction if we are going to use it to guide us.***

Application: When we are trying to find our way through the journey of life, God has given us a spiritual compass to guide our path. That guide is the Bible, God's Holy Word.

The truth that we find in the Bible never changes. It will always point us in the same direction. It will always point us to Jesus.

Some people use their feelings to help them to decide what they should do. That's no good. Our feelings change from day to day, and they cannot be trusted. Besides that, just because we feel good about something doesn't mean that it is the right thing to do.

Some people choose what they will do by what's popular. That is no good either. Just because everyone else is doing it doesn't mean that it is the right thing to do, does it? Tomorrow everyone might be doing something else.

Some people even put blind trust in science and believe everything they read in textbooks and magazines because scientists are really intelligent and seem to have the answers.

There is only one thing that we can trust to **always** point us in the right direction, and that is the Bible. It will always point to Jesus, and Jesus said "I am the way, the truth, and the life, and no man comes to the Father but by me."

The Bible is the compass for our life. We can always depend on God's Word to point us in the right direction.

1. Have the students turn to the front of their workbooks at this time. Use a minute or two to familiarize them with the contents of this study. Have them look over the Table of Contents and briefly flip through the book. Let them know there will be some required and some optional "homework." Share an incentive idea with them (and get their ideas for incentives) to encourage them to put forth effort into getting the most out of this study.
2. Have everyone turn to the Introduction to the workbook. Call on individuals to read parts of the paragraph aloud, then ask for comments.
3. Call on individuals to read the Introduction for Lesson 1. Take a minute or two to discuss this information.
4. Read the Scripture passage while the students follow along, then have everyone read it together. Let them know that they will be working on one verse per week and that throughout this 13-lesson course, you will be studying each verse in more depth.

HANDOUT

The handout for this lesson is *Biblical Authority Unleashed*. You have several options for how to utilize it.

- Read and discuss briefly with the group.
- Assign for reading to discuss next week.
- Take a full lesson time to read, discuss, and refer to Scripture references.
- Cover a small section of it over the next few lessons.

Be sure to emphasize to your students that they should read and refer to this chart often until they can verbalize much of its contents.

Instruct the students to turn to Lesson 1 in their Student Workbooks and in their Bibles to 2 Timothy 4. Call on an individual to read verses 1 and 2. Call on others to read or read to them the following introductory information. Students should follow along in their workbooks.

Transition idea: Use a video clip from "Passion of the Christ" where Jesus is brought before Pilot re: "What is truth?" (Time code 38:55–42:59)

Make sure all participants have something to write with so that they can actively participate during the DVD presentation.

WAR OF THE WORLDVIEWS PART 1

CAN WE REALLY TRUST THE BIBLE?

LAYING THE GROUNDWORK

2 Timothy 4:2 begins by saying, "Preach the word." The "WORD" in this verse is the Word of God, the Scriptures, the Holy Bible, and that's what this series is about — sharing the TRUTH of God's Word with a lost, deceived, disillusioned world. But how do we know if what God's Word says really is the TRUTH?

In this lesson you will be given evidence, data, and historical facts that confirm the authenticity of the Bible. You'll find out what biblical Christians believe about the world around them (their worldview) and how we as Christians can support our beliefs about the Bible and the origin of the world.

Before watching the DVD, however, let's define some terms.

Doctrine—a rule or principle that forms the basis of belief; a body of ideas taught to people as truthful or correct

Epistemology—the branch of Western philosophy that studies the nature and scope of knowledge and belief

Origins—the study of the beginning of time, matter, and life

Revelation—God's disclosure of Himself and His will to His creatures

Truth—being in accord with experience, facts, or reality; accuracy

World—secular or social life and interests as opposed to spiritual life

Worldview—how one views and interprets the world around him

Culture—the ideas, customs, etc. of a given people in a given period

5

DEMOLISHING STRONGHOLDS

VIEW THE DVD

(Watch for the key thoughts that complete the statements below and fill them in as you watch and listen.)

In America right now, people talk about the fact that there's a culture war. The creation— evolution issue is foundational to the culture war … a war between two worldviews.

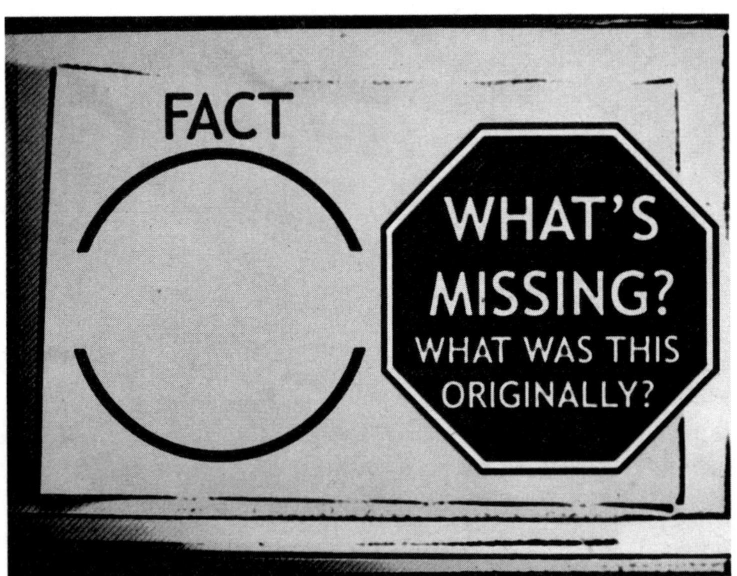

Answers will vary.

What happened in the past to produce this [shape]?

In the topic of origins, what we're trying to do is to say, "How do we connect the present to the past?"

The message of evolution: "When you die, that's the end of you."

The message of the Bible: "God so loved the world, He gave His only begotten Son that whoever believes in Him should not perish, but have everlasting life."

6 

Following each video presentation, feel free to draw out key points and get feedback from the students. We have built in about 5–7 minutes in this section for such discussion.

DEMOLISHING STRONGHOLDS

Creationists and evolutionists all have the same earth, same fossils, same animals, same rock layers and canyons, same world, etc . . . We all have the same facts. The real battle is over the same evidence.

However, we have two different interpretations of the facts.

When we put on biblical glasses, we learn that revelation is the key to the past and the present.

Presuppositions (foundational starting points) if my worldview starts with God and the Bible:

1. Life is the result of intelligence (God).

   DNA shows evidence of an intelligence (DNA is actually an information system—a code. Scientists know codes only come from an intelligence, and information only comes from information. Nobody's ever seen a code or information arise from matter.)

2. Fossils and rock layers are consistent with a catastrophic global flood.

3. The human genome maps show there's only one race. Evidence is inconsistent with the idea of humans arising from ape-like ancestors and different races (evolution).

DEMOLISHING STRONGHOLDS

WHAT DO YOU MEAN BY . . .

Science: knowledge ; it is observable, testable, and repeatable.

Faith: firm belief in something for which there is no proof .

Religion: a cause, a principle, a system of belief held to with honor and faith .

GET INTO THE WORD

Let's take a closer look at key words used in the following verses. Throughout the next week, take the challenge of digging even deeper into the message and power of this passage.

2 Timothy 3:16-17

Inspiration: "God-breathed" God literally breathed into the human authors the words He wanted mankind to receive.

Doctrine: "teachings" A rule or principle that forms the basis of belief.

Complete: "mature" We need nothing more than God's complete Word for our complete life.

Discuss:

1. In light of Paul's purpose for writing to Timothy, why do you think he was guided by the Holy Spirit to assert the authority of the Scripture?

   One of the first things that Satan will use to weaken God's message is an attack on the authenticity of God's Word (See Genesis 3 where Satan causes Eve to

Have the students turn in their Bibles to 2 Timothy 3:16–17.

Discuss the meaning of the words *Inspiration*, *Doctrine*, and *Complete*.

You may use the PowerPoint slides as you work through this section.

Discuss the questions and feel free to add additional insight as time allows.

Read and discuss the quotation by Dr. David Noebel.

DEMOLISHING STRONGHOLDS

question and twist what God had said.) If God is not true to His Word, then why should we trust Him? With this message in Paul's letter, Timothy now had the Word of God affirmed and confirmed.

2. What Scripture is being referred to in these verses?

   All Scripture in the original manuscripts. (It's important for teenagers to understand that Bible Study in which they can access the original Hebrew and Greek meanings is essential to deep study of God's Word and will lead to spiritual maturity.)

3. What are some of the doctrines you have learned since becoming a Christian?

   Answers will vary but may include topics such as the Person and Work of Christ, God's Attributes, the Scriptures, Sacraments, Future Events, Angels, Heaven, etc ...

> "Christianity explains the facts of reality better than any other worldview **because it relies upon divine inspiration**. If the Bible is truly God's special revelation to man, as we believe it is, then the only completely accurate view of the world must be founded on Scripture."
>
> —*The Battle for Truth* by Dr. David Noebel, p. 18

ADDITIONAL THOUGHTS

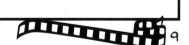

9

DEMOLISHING STRONGHOLDS

FIND THE FOCUS

Whenever God gives us new information or repeats something we've heard in the past, He wants us to pay attention. Think for a moment ... look back over the notes you have for this lesson, and write down a couple of things that were an encouragement or a challenge, or that stood out to you. (Ideas: Maybe you were made more aware of why you believe or should believe that the Bible is the **only** holy, inspired Word of God; or maybe it became apparent to you through Ken's talk that science—true science—and the Bible are on the same page.)

Whatever you write, be specific and be prepared to share it with the group.

1. ______________________________
____
____
____
____

2. ______________________________
____
____
____
____

HOMEWORK

1. Memorize 2 Timothy 4:1.
2. Read over the article "Biblical Authority Unleashed" several times and be prepared to share three items you could use to defend the authenticity and accuracy of the Bible.

10 

During this part of the lesson, it is important to give the teens "alone" time to really meditate on the lesson. If they have the option of spreading out or going to other areas, it might be beneficial to encourage this. Give them a time limit. If at this point in the lesson you have run out of time, add it to their homework and tell them to fill it in to share next week.

You may find that assigning the *Find the Focus* section would be more effectively utilized as part of the homework so that the students truly have "alone" time in which to reflect upon the lesson.

Hand out the article, "Biblical Authority Unleashed" located on the CD-Rom.

See the CD-Rom for the *Optional Activity* for this lesson.

WAR OF THE WORLDVIEWS PART 2

ASKING THE RIGHT QUESTIONS

OVERVIEW

As Ken continues to lay the foundation for this study, he exposes more of the traps Christians can fall into if they are not properly educated regarding the nature of the spiritual battle. It's not between science and the Bible; rather, it's between evolution and the Bible.

OBJECTIVES

As a result of this lesson, students will be able to:

1. Define and give an example of an axiom/pre-supposition.
2. Summarize the "straw man" concept.
3. Define evolution in two ways.
4. Compare/contrast the Gospel versus the anti-gospel.

BEFORE THE LESSON

Opening Prayer, Announcements, etc.

Review the *Homework*

As a group, read the entire memory passage together.

Then, have the students divide into small groups of five. Each person in each group gets a turn to recite 2 Timothy 4:1. Once completed, the students should form one large group again.

Ask for several volunteers to share three items from the "Biblical Authority Unleashed" information to defend the authenticity of the Bible. Be sure to praise them for a job well done.

Object Lesson: 20 Questions

Choose a student to be in the "Hot Seat." Tell him/her to think of a person, place, or thing for the others to guess and to secretly tell you what it is before the game begins.

Instruct the rest of the group that they can ask a total of 20 questions to the "Hot Seat" to try to figure out what the word is. All questions must be able to be answered with a "yes" or a "no."

Application: "In order for you to find out the exact word that ____________ had chosen, your questions had to lead to the right conclusion. One of the tasks before us as Christians is to ask the right questions to unbelievers to get them to come to the right conclusions about origins, life and death, etc. The truth of the claims of God's Word can be revealed through questions that can only logically be answered by the Scriptures."

HANDOUT

Many students have no idea how much science is included in the Bible. The handout for this lesson, *Science and the Scriptures,* is an excellent resource for both you and your students.

WAR OF THE WORLDVIEWS PART 2

CAN WE REALLY TRUST THE BIBLE?

LAYING THE GROUNDWORK

In 2 Timothy 4:2b, we are commanded to "Be ready in season and out of season. Convince, rebuke, exhort, with all longsuffering and teaching."

Let's read how the Amplified Bible explains this verse and think about it a little more personally:

"Keep your sense of urgency [stand by, be at hand and ready]..."

- Do you live each day as if it could be your last?
- Do your choices show that you are ready, willing, and able to speak up for the Lord without advance notice?
- Are you ready in the sense of knowing what you believe and why you believe it?
- Are you ready to defend your faith in relation to salvation, creation, daily life, etc.?

"...whether the opportunity seems to be favorable or unfavorable. [Whether it is convenient or inconvenient, whether it is welcome or unwelcome, you as preacher of the Word are to show people in what way their lives are wrong.]"

- Do you avoid being in conversations/situations in which your beliefs might be questioned or attacked?
- Do you know how to present your beliefs using God's Word so that He can use His Word to convict others of the truth?

11

Instruct the students to turn to Lesson 2 in their Student Workbooks. Call on an individual to read the first sentence. Have the whole group read the Amplified verse segments, then you read the questions, pausing where appropriate. Students should follow along in their workbooks.

Make sure all participants have something to write with so that they can actively participate during the DVD presentation.

DEMOLISHING STRONGHOLDS

"And convince them, rebuking and correcting, warning and urging and encouraging them, being unflagging and inexhaustible in patience and teaching."

- Do you have a concern and compassion for others and understand the urgency of reaching them for Christ?
- Do you pray for your unsaved friends regularly?
- Do you live your life so that others see Jesus Christ in your thoughts, words, and actions?

Are you prepared for spiritual battle? The commands presented in this verse are a sobering reminder that we need to ready ourselves by understanding our enemy and his tactics. In this lesson, you will be made aware of how evolutionists and evolutionary textbooks try to lead you to unbiblical conclusions about origins. You will also see clear evidence presented that supports biblical creation and be reminded of the fact that the Bible confirms what true science shows.

Before watching the DVD, however, let's define some terms.

Presupposition: A starting point accepted as true; an established principle or law of science, art, etc.

Straw Man: As a rhetorical term, "straw man" describes a point of view that was created *in order to be easily defeated in argument*; the creator of a "straw man" argument does not accurately reflect the best arguments of his or her opponents, but instead sidesteps or mischaracterizes them so as *to make the opposing view appear weak or ridiculous.*

> An example of this is when person A says "I don't think children should run into the busy streets." Person B responds "I think that it would be foolish to lock up children all day with no fresh air." This insinuates that person A's argument is ridiculous and far more severe or extreme than it is.

12 

DEMOLISHING STRONGHOLDS

VIEW THE DVD

(Watch for the key thoughts that complete the statements below and fill them in as you watch and listen.)

How do you find out who's __right__ [about origins]?

We can use __observational__ science and apply it to those interpretations of facts.

When we apply observational science to changes in dogs, it really confirms biblical __kinds__ because dogs __remain__ dogs, elephants remain __elephants__, etc. There's __NO__ evidence of a mechanism to change one __kind__ into another when you study genetics. When you study __fossils__ and you study the rock layers, actually what you find over the earth is more consistent with __catastrophic__ processes, NOT __millions__ of years of processes.

Definition #1 for Evolution—Dictionary definition: a process of __change__ in a certain direction; an unfolding; i.e., __change__.

True or False

"Before Charles Darwin, most people believed that God created all living things in exactly the form we see them today. This is the basis of the doctrine of creation." (Quotation from a display in the *Natural History Museum* in London, England)

BEWARE OF THE STRAW MAN!

The evolution they are referring to is __molecules__-to-__man__ evolution, but all they define it as is __change__. People get indoctrinated here!

What Darwin observed was not a process of __change__ that would change one kind into __another__; he observed the hand of __God__ in the phenomenal __variability__ that God placed there.

__Observational__ science and __genetics__ confirm the Bible's account of kinds; it __doesn't__ confirm molecules-to-man evolution! The Bible's history is __true__!

YOUR STARTING POINT DETERMINES YOUR WHOLE __WORLDVIEW__!

13

Following each video presentation, feel free to draw out key points and get feedback from the students. We have built in about 5-7 minutes in this section for such discussion.

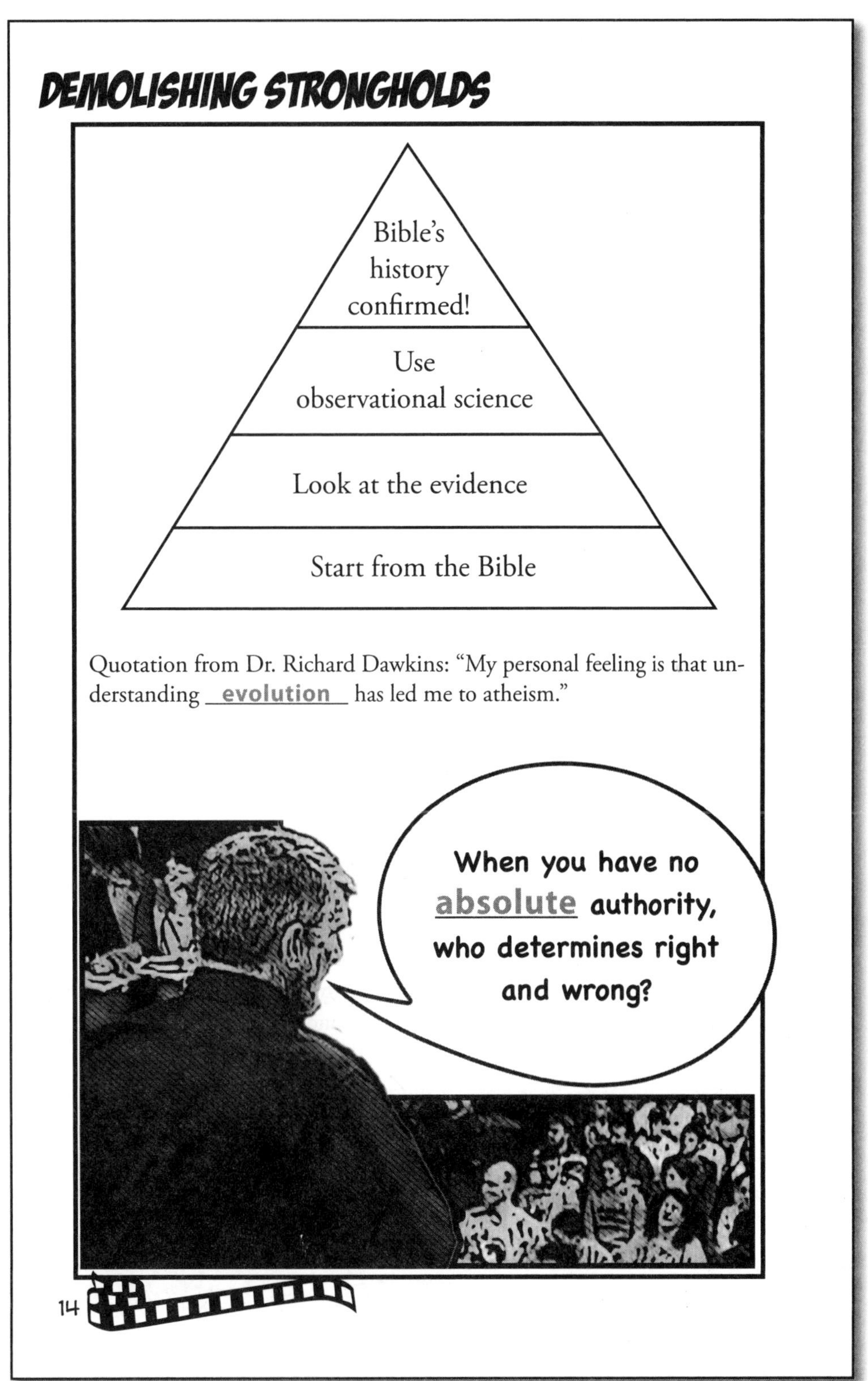
DEMOLISHING STRONGHOLDS
Bible's history confirmed!
Use observational science
Look at the evidence
Start from the Bible
Quotation from Dr. Richard Dawkins: "My personal feeling is that understanding evolution has led me to atheism."
When you have no absolute authority, who determines right and wrong?
14

DEMOLISHING STRONGHOLDS

DEMOLISHING STRONGHOLDS

The worldview battle is really a battle between the __Gospel__ and the anti-gospel.

Gospel	Anti-gospel
"the __good__ news"	Man is just an __animal.__
Jesus died on the cross & was raised from the dead for __our sin.__	When you die, that's it.
__God's Word__ is truth.	__Man__ determines truth.

GET INTO THE WORD

Read **Romans 1:19–20** and **Psalm 19:1**, then be ready to respond to the following items:

1. Discuss and write down two or three things that God has shown you in His creation to indicate He is the eternal Creator.

____

____

____

____

____

2. How do the "heavens declare the glory of God"? Give an example.

____

____

____

____

____

3. The phrase "without excuse" is literally, "without an apologetic" or "without a defense" (Greek *apologia*—the same word used for "answer" in 1 Peter 3:15). As Ken pointed out in this session, there

15

Have the students turn to these passages in their Bibles. Call on individuals to read or read to them while they follow along in their Bibles. Remind them to keep their place in these two references should they need to refer back to them to answer the questions. The answers to questions 1 & 3 will be variable and students may need your guidance.

Note: Even though people instinctively know there is a God by looking at creation (Psalm 19; Romans 1), they still must be told what His name is. It is not enough to simply know and believe there is a Creator—we must know Him by name—thus, the Gospel.

During this part of the lesson each week, it is important to give the teens "alone" time to really meditate on the lesson. If they have the option of spreading out or going to other areas, it might be beneficial to encourage this. Give them a time limit. If at this point in the lesson, you have run out of time, add it to their homework assignment and tell them to fill it in to share next week.

DEMOLISHING STRONGHOLDS

is absolutely no evidence to support molecules-to-man evolution. In contrast, the evidence for creation is all around us. Discuss with the group and write down several examples that provide additional evidence of the divine creation.

____

____

____

____

Note: Even though people instinctively know there is a God (Psalm 19; Romans 1) by looking at creation, they still must be told what His name is. It is not enough to simply know and believe there is a Creator—we must know Him by name—thus, the Gospel.

ADDITIONAL THOUGHTS

____

____

____

____

____

FIND THE FOCUS

Whenever God gives us new information or repeats something we've heard in the past, He wants us to pay attention. Think for a moment … look back over the notes you have for this lesson, and write down a couple of things that were an encouragement or a challenge, or that stood out to you. (Ideas: Maybe you were made more aware of how you have been indoctrinated by humanistic thought, or maybe it became apparent to you through Ken's talk that evolution is not supported by science but is a "blind faith" religion.)

Whatever you write, be specific and be prepared to share it with the group.

16 

DEMOLISHING STRONGHOLDS

DEMOLISHING STRONGHOLDS

1. ____

2. ____

HOMEWORK

1. Memorize 2 Timothy 4:2. Practice saying verses 1 and 2 together.
2. Complete any part of the lesson that you were not able to finish in class. Be prepared to discuss your answers.
3. Read Ephesians 4:14–15 and 2 Thessalonians 2:1–12 to prepare your heart for next week's Bible focus.

17

Hand out the chart, "Science and the Scriptures" located on the CD-Rom. Instead of going through the whole chart with them, pick two or three items to look up to see how science is confirmed in the Scriptures.

You may want to use the PowerPoint slides as you work through this section.

See the CD-Rom for the *Optional Activity* for this lesson.

EVOLUTION IN POP CULTURE PART 1

WHAT'S WRONG WITH IT?

OVERVIEW

How much TV do you think the average person watches in a week? Research shows that the average child watches about 1,023 hours of TV each year! That's more than is spent in school! Additionally, children are exposed to approximately 40,000 ads via the television as well. With all of this visual media they're exposed to, it's not difficult to understand how worldliness and worldly values are "absorbed" by them even in good Christian homes. Understanding that an overwhelming majority of shows and movies are produced by unbelievers who have adopted the evolutionist worldview, it is natural to assume that their personal philosophies will reveal themselves in these programs. In these next two lessons, Carl Kerby, Vice President of Ministry Relations at AiG and a well-known AiG speaker, will show multiple examples of how children and teenagers are exposed to evolution and other worldly philosophies through television and movies.

OBJECTIVES

As a result of this lesson, students will be able to:

Identify the quantity of evolutionary ideas presented in viewed television over a week's time.

Recognize the influence that the media have on our lives by giving 2 or 3 examples of messages received via TV, radio, or movies that are contrary to biblical principles.

Describe how Lot was drawn into the worldly influences of Sodom and Gomorrah

(Genesis 13:8–9).

Explain the role of science fiction in the media.

BEFORE THE LESSON

Opening Prayer, Announcements, etc.

Review the *Homework*

As a group, read the entire memory passage together.

Then, have the students divide into small groups of five. Each person in each group gets a turn to recite 2 Timothy 4:1–2. Once completed, the students should form one large group again.

If there was unfinished material from the last lessons, ask for several volunteers to share their answers.

Briefly review another point or two from the "Biblical Authority Unleashed" chart from Lesson 1 and encourage them to continue getting to know this information.

Object Lesson: Do you know the real thing when you see it?

Materials needed: Have a new dollar bill to show

Illustration – Counterfeit money

According to the Federal Reserve, the government organization responsible for production and distribution of money, the best way to detect counterfeit money is to know all the facts about *genuine* US Currency. Just as criminals try to manufacture fake bills to profit, so Satan will use false information through the array of secular television shows and movies to deceive us into believing we have received valid information. How can we guard our hearts and minds from being misled by these ideas? First and foremost, we need to know the real thing—God's Word and its truths. When we know and understand the biblical worldview, other philosophies will be easy to detect. Today's lesson will help us identify some of the evolutionary thoughts portrayed in several commonly watched television shows.

Note: If you have access to a computer with internet and can project it onto a screen, log on to www.youthonline.ca/games/difference/ and choose one of the items for your youth to compare. It's much harder than it looks. The first illustration is the "real thing" while the second has several subtle variations on it.

Application: Sometimes the counterfeit is so close to the real thing that it can be easy to miss its subtle differences. As Christians, we need to be on our guard for subtle variations from Scripture and the biblical worldview.

Have all the participants turn in their workbooks to Lesson 3, "Laying the Groundwork." Call on an individual to read the Scripture verse. Pick up from there by reading the rest of the text in this section while they follow along in their books.

HANDOUT

This handout for this week includes invaluable information for helping your teenagers develop another way of studying the Bible. Many people don't study the Bible consistently either because they don't know how or they haven't been introduced to a method that is easy for them to put into practice.

Through the rest of this study, your students will be using portions of the Inductive Bible Study Method. Following this study, you may want to lead a study of Genesis, one of the epistles, or the book of Proverbs using this method to give them additional practice.

Part of the *Homework* for this week will be to read through the handout thoroughly to prepare for next week. With that in mind, you may simply want to highlight some of the key points in this section as a culmination of this lesson. The handout is located on the CD-Rom.

Instruct the students to turn to Lesson 3 in their Student Workbooks. Call on an individual to read the first sentence. Have the whole group read the Amplified verse segments, then you read the questions, pausing where appropriate. Students should follow along in their workbooks.

Make sure all participants have something to write with so that they can actively participate during the DVD presentation.

EVOLUTION IN POP CULTURE PART 1

WHAT'S WRONG WITH IT?

LAYING THE GROUNDWORK

In 2 Timothy 4:3, we are warned, "For the time will come when they will not endure sound doctrine, but according to their own desires, because they have itching ears, they will heap up for themselves teachers."

Once again, the Amplified Bible can provide a detailed commentary on the content presented in this verse:

> For the time is coming when [people] will not tolerate (endure) sound and wholesome instruction, but, having ears itching [for something pleasing and gratifying], they will gather to themselves one teacher after another to a considerable number, chosen to satisfy their own liking and to foster the errors they hold...

Discuss and answer the following questions with the group and ask God to prepare your heart for the message He has for you in today's lesson.

What "time" does this verse remind you of?

The present day world

Where can you go for sound doctrine? How do you know this?

The Bible; God's Word is truth; 2 Timothy 3:16 says "All scripture is profitable for ...doctrine." They might add in ideas from the chart in Lesson 1 as well.

In this lesson, you will come face to face with some of the false teachings presented to you in TV shows and movies you may watch or may

18 

DEMOLISHING STRONGHOLDS

have watched. The intent of this session is to get you excited about really getting to know God and His Word. We need to be equipped to stand against the obstacles that humanists and non-Christians use to try to trip us up. Knowing what you believe and why you believe it will enable you to develop the mind of Christ and overpower the influence of the media in your life.

VIEW THE DVD

(Watch for the key thoughts that complete the statements below and fill them in as you watch and listen.)

We as the body of Christ have to start getting __excited__ about our __faith__. We need to get out into the __public__ and start __impacting__ people.

Evangelism is a __conversation__ not a presentation. Are you __conversing__? To do that we need to understand the way that the world is seeing us and how we can break down those __barriers__ that keep us from being able to have __real__ conversations with people (2 Corinthians 10:4–5).

The very first step in being able to be real with people and to talk with people and to have conversations with people is to __recognize__ there's a __problem__ going on.

Without recognition there can be no __resolution__.

"It is time to recognize that the true tutors of our children are not school teachers or university professors but __film makers__, __advertising__ executives, and __pop culture__ purveyors. __Disney__ does more than Duke, __Spielberg__ outweighs Stanford, __MTV__ trumps MIT."—University of Maryland Professor

Lot's Fall into Worldliness (Genesis 13:8–9)

1. "He lifted up his eyes." – Lot looked around with his __physical__ eyes. He used his physical eyes to make a very important __decision__ (Proverbs 3:7; 16:25).

19

DEMOLISHING STRONGHOLDS

Application: When you and I use our physical eyes, we use *our* wisdom; we can be __deceived__ because the world can make things look really __good__.

2. "He pitched his tent towards Sodom." – Lot didn't live in the city because he wanted the best of both worlds.

3. In chapter 19 Lot's living __within__ the city walls! –Years had passed between chapters 13 and 19; He didn't get sucked in all at once; it was a slow, gradual __process__.

Application: What happens to us is many times we get sucked into the world:

Slowly and gradually we start __adopting__ the ways of the world.

We start __looking like__ the world.

We start __reflecting__ the world's standards instead of the Word's standards.

KEY THOUGHT

"The vast majority of Christians do not behave differently because they do not __think__ differently, and they do not think differently because we've never __trained__ them, __equipped__ them, or held them accountable to do so."

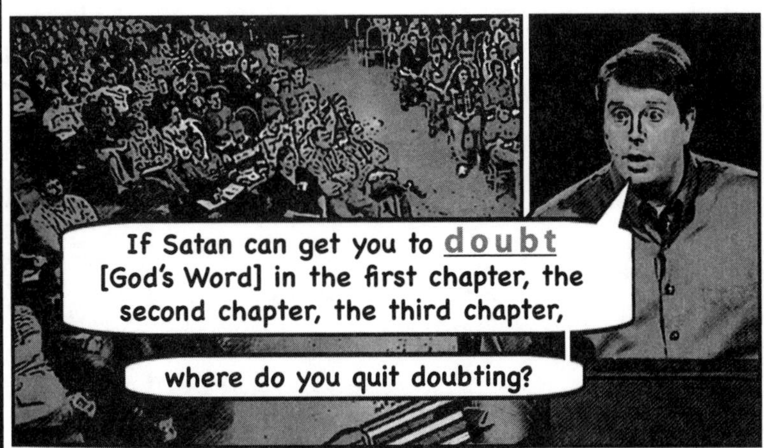

If Satan can get you to doubt [God's Word] in the first chapter, the second chapter, the third chapter,
where do you quit doubting?

20

DEMOLISHING STRONGHOLDS

The Bible is like a __radar__ system and if you don't use it properly, you're not going to like the __results__ that you get.

Satan's tool that's being used on our culture today to get us to doubt is __millions of years__ and evolution.

***Watch as Carl shares several clips from TV shows/movies that support evolutionary thought.*

CARL'S OBSERVATION ABOUT SCIENCE FICTION

Science fiction is a __bridge__. You do not get from "There is a God" to "There is no God" just like that most of the time. There has to be a bridge—you can believe in God, He just used evolution; He just directed the Big Bang.

Opportunities (or obstacles?) for biblical conversations

Messages from the Media through:

Advertising　　Movies

TV　　Music

Internet

Recognize that when you open up your mind [when] watching a movie, you open up your mind to the messages inside of those movies. Be discerning and confront these messages with the Truth!

GET INTO THE WORD

Read Ephesians 4:14–15; 2 Thessalonians 2:1–12.

Discuss and answer the following items:

1. What does the word "deceive" mean in these passages?

   To mislead—to cause to follow the wrong course

2. Who is constantly trying to deceive us? What tactics does he use?

   Satan; causes us to doubt God's Word, uses powers,

21

Have the students turn to these passages in their Bibles. Call on individuals to read or read to them while they follow along in their Bibles. Remind them to keep their place in these two references should they need to refer back to them to answer the questions. The answers will vary and students may need your guidance.

You may want to use the PowerPoint slides for this section.

During this part of the lesson each week, it is important to give the teens "alone" time to really meditate on the lesson. If they have the option of spreading out or going to other areas, it might be beneficial to encourage this. Give them a time limit. If at this point in the lesson, you have run out of time, add it to their homework assignment and tell them to fill it in to share next week.

DEMOLISHING STRONGHOLDS

signs, and lying wonders; deceives us into committing acts of unrighteousness

3. According to Jeremiah 17:9 and James 1:14, what else can we be deceived by?

   Our hearts

4. Name one or two things you can do to avoid being deceived by evolution's lies.

   Study God's Word so that we know the truth; know the enemy and be aware of his tactics; Pray for God's wisdom and discernment.

Throughout the next week, take the challenge of digging even deeper into the message and power of this passage.

ADDITIONAL THOUGHTS

____

____

____

____

FIND THE FOCUS

Whenever God gives us new information or repeats something we've heard in the past, He wants us to pay attention. Think for a moment … look back over the notes you have for this lesson, and write down a couple of things that were an encouragement or a challenge, or that stood out to you.

1. ______________________________

   ____

   ____

22

DEMOLISHING STRONGHOLDS

2. ____

HOMEWORK

1. Memorize 2 Timothy 4:3. Practice saying verses 1–3 together.
2. Complete any part of the lesson that you were not able to finish in class. Be prepared to discuss your answers.
3. Read through the entire article on Inductive Bible Study before next week's lesson. Ask God to prepare your heart for deeper study of His Word.
4. Pre-read 2 Corinthians 10 and 2 Timothy 2 to prepare your heart for next week's Bible focus.

23

Hand out the article, "Developing a Biblical Worldview Through Inductive Bible Study" located on the CD-Rom. You may want to go over the main points with your students and encourage them to read it through and use it.

You may use the PowerPoint slides for this section.

See the CD-Rom for the *Optional Activity* for this lesson .

EVOLUTION IN POP CULTURE PART 2

WHAT ARE YOU TALKING ABOUT?

OVERVIEW

In this lesson, Carl Kerby focuses on the evolution portrayed in movies, especially science fiction movies. He presents information that shows how science fiction became a bridge between "there-is-a-God" and "there-is-no-God" thinking in the twentieth century. He concludes with a powerful appeal for teenagers to know ***why*** they believe what they believe so that they can answer the difficult questions they may encounter. To help the participants begin to acquire more of this godly wisdom, the final section of this lesson includes an explanation from Ken Ham for the much-asked question: "Why is there death and suffering?"

OBJECTIVES

As a result of this lesson, students will be able to:

1. Identify several of the evolutionary thoughts presented in the movie clips Carl uses.
2. Explain a crucial fault in the Intelligent Design model in relation to eternity. (Phil. 2:9–11)
3. Define "syncretism."
4. Present the Gospel in an informal group setting initiated by regular conversation.

BEFORE THE LESSON

Opening Prayer, Announcements, etc.

Review the *Homework*

1. As a group, read the entire memory passage together.
2. Then, have the students divide into small groups of five. Each person in each group gets a turn to recite 2 Timothy 4:1–3. Once completed, the students should form one large group again.
3. If there was unfinished material from the last lessons, ask for several volunteers to share their answers.

Object Lesson: Balderdash!

True or False

Participants will need a small piece of paper or a 3x5 card to write on. Have them number it from 1–5. They will write only True or False beside each number.

You will be conducting a quick version of a bluffing game like "Balderdash" or "Malarky." Using the words given below, you will give the students the "definition" of each, and they must decide if your definition is "true" or "false," Go through these like a quiz—simply making the statement and having them write "true" or "false" for it. Once all have been given, go back over them to check them and share the correct answer.

DEMOLISHING STRONGHOLDS

Do a tally by raise of hands to determine who got #1 correct, #2 correct, etc.

True or False: A malkin is another word for a scarecrow. (T)

True or False: Pocosin is the name given to a low-lying section of the Appalachian Mountains located in eastern Pennsylvania. (F) A pocosin is a low, flat, swampy region in the savannas of the SE United States.

True or False: Scotoma is a form of cancer that forms in the eyes. (F) A scotoma is a dark area or gap in the visual field.

True or False: A screak is another word for a screech. (T)

True or False: A budgerigar is an Australian parakeet. (T)

Application: There are two twists on this game.

1. If you were able to fool them on any of the items, say this: "All I had to do to fool you was to sound smart and act like I knew what I was talking about since you were not familiar with the word. It was that easy to get you to believe something that wasn't true. When you encounter an evolutionist, such as a science teacher, you are in a better situation than I put you in just now. You have the tools/materials needed to understand where he's coming from and the ability to increase your knowledge base so that you can ask intelligent questions to get him to show the evidence for what he believes; most likely, there will be none."

2. If you were not able to fool them (not likely, but possible), say this: "Because I wasn't able to fool you with these words, that tells me one of two things—either you already had the knowledge necessary to accurately answer these statements, or you are very good guessers. If the first is true, I want to challenge you to increase your knowledge on the issue of a biblical worldview so that you know what you believe and why you believe it. That's really the only way you are going to be able to stand against the humanistic worldview you're surrounded by. If you're just a really good guesser, that won't carry you too far in life. Eventually you will guess wrong, and it could end up causing you to doubt your faith or make you look unprepared to answer tough questions. Remember, the opposition is often *well* prepared to defend their 'faith.'"

HANDOUT

One of the thoughts Carl Kerby presented in his talk on "Evolution in Pop Culture" was that people may not listen to you if all you present is a God of love who has a wonderful plan for your life (i.e., you may have to answer some tough questions). The handout for this week will help your students to get a good start in that direction so that they can prepare to "give a defense to everyone who asks you a reason for the hope that is in you, with meekness and fear" (1 Peter 3:15).

This handout is located on the supplementary CD-Rom.

Have the students turn to Lesson 4 "Laying the Groundwork" in their student workbooks. Instruct them to read 1 Peter 3:15 with you. Immediately begin reading the remainder of this section while they follow along.

Make sure all participants have something to write with so that they can actively participate during the DVD presentation.

EVOLUTION IN POP CULTURE PART 2

WHAT ARE YOU TALKING ABOUT?

LAYING THE GROUNDWORK

1 Peter 3:15 says "But sanctify the Lord God in your hearts, and always be ready to give a defense to everyone who asks you a reason for the hope that is in you, with meekness and fear."

By this time in the study of *Demolishing Strongholds*, you should be beginning to identify worldly influences in your day-to-day life. More importantly, you are becoming more aware of the false teachings perpetrated in the media and the humanistic worldview from which they stem.

Your challenge in this lesson will be to do something about the worldly influences in your life. This may include "raising the bar" in your viewing standards (TV/movies), pointing out the humanistic/evolutionary influences to fellow believers, and/or confronting the culture head-on to make an impact for Christ. Whatever role God may have you play, it will necessitate the need for really knowing His Word and knowing how to answer some of the tough questions non-Christians might come up with.

Before watching the DVD, however, let's define some terms.

New Age: a broad movement of late twentieth-century and contemporary Western culture, characterized by an individual eclectic approach to spiritual exploration.

Syncretism: the attempt to reconcile opposing beliefs and to meld practices of various schools of thought; i.e., in the realm of religion to say that there are many ways to get to Heaven so that no one is offended.

24 

DEMOLISHING STRONGHOLDS

DEMOLISHING STRONGHOLDS

Wicca: the polytheistic nature religion of modern witchcraft whose central deity is a mother goddess. Wicca incorporate a specific form of witchcraft, with particular ritual forms, involving the casting of spells, herbalism, divination, and other magic.

VIEW THE DVD

Much of Carl's video presentation for this lesson is focused on movie clips. Though there will not be many notes to fill in, the ones chosen are to the point and powerful.

Be careful with Intelligent Design . . ., because unless you name the Name [of Jesus], the designer's not going to get you into Heaven. Jesus Christ—at the name of Jesus every knee shall bow and tongue confess. . ."

There's something that's even better than spider sense. It's called **Bible** sense.

- God has given us a **record**.
- He's the only one who's **always** been there.
- He's given us a **true history** book to be able to deal with the world that we're living in.

You can have Bible sense when you **start** from the Word of God to **understand** the world that we live in, to have **answers** to real issues.

We've been trained to put on those glasses to think like the **world**. Think about it.

- Average time a child in America spends in school = **900 hrs. per year**
- Average time a child in America spends in front of the television set = **1,023 hrs. per year**
- Average time we spend in church = **2–3 hours per week** (about 100–150 hrs. per year)

25

Following each video presentation, feel free to draw out key points and get feedback from the students. We have built in about 5–7 minutes in this section for such discussion.

DEMOLISHING STRONGHOLDS

Have students turn to these passages in their Bibles and hand out "Original Greek of Key Words" (located on the CD-Rom).

Call on individuals to read *or* read to them while they follow along in their Bibles.

Remind them to keep their place in these two references should they need to refer back to them to answer the questions.

Ask them to put the context of the passage into a sentence. Give them a few minutes in small groups to come up with concise sentences, then join as a large group to go over the items.

DEMOLISHING STRONGHOLDS

IN ORDER TO CONFRONT THE CULTURE

Trust the Word of God completely from the first verse. Use it as a real solid foundation.

You need to have a reasonable, rational explanation of why you believe what you believe.

> "Scripture, not science, is the ultimate test of all truth and the further evangelicalism gets from that conviction, the less evangelical and the more humanistic it becomes."
> —Dr. John MacArthur

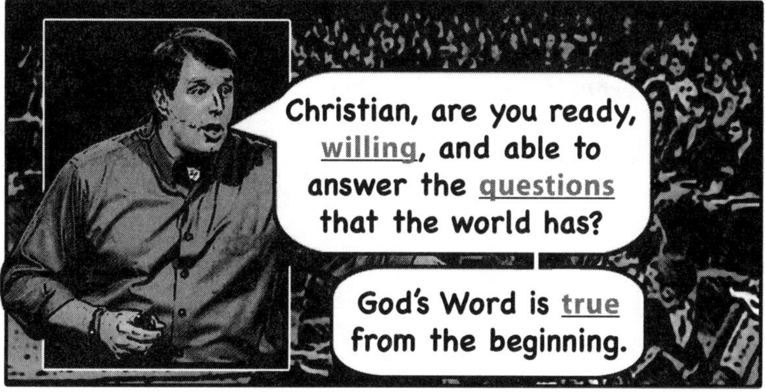

Christian, are you ready, willing, and able to answer the questions that the world has?
God's Word is true from the beginning.

We need to get equipped and start thinking from the Word of God—with no apologies, and have answers from the Word of God—*using* the culture, not being abused by the culture.

GET INTO THE WORD

2 Corinthians 10:3–5; 2 Timothy 2:15

Beginning with this lesson, our Scripture passage will be covered in much more detail as we work through the Inductive Bible Study process. Your assignment from last week was to read the context passages of our Scripture verses for this lesson, so we'll begin by discussing the overview of the passage.

26

DEMOLISHING STRONGHOLDS

2 Corinthians 10: **When glory is given, it should all go to the Lord.**

2 Timothy 2: **There are two main themes of this chapter: "Endure hardness as a good soldier" and "Study to show thyself approved unto God."**

Now let's take a closer look at the key verses. We'll answer as many of the six questions as we can, and we'll look for key words.

2 Corinthians 10:3–5

"For though we walk in the flesh, we do not war according to the flesh. For the weapons of our warfare are not carnal but mighty in God for pulling down strongholds, casting down arguments and every high thing that exalts itself against the knowledge of God, bringing every thought into captivity to the obedience of Christ."

Who? **These verses are directed toward us; we need to pay close attention here. God—He's the one who provides our way of escape and arms us for the battle.**

What? **We're in spiritual warfare. We have spiritual weapons. We need to keep our thoughts in Christ's control.**

When? **Presently—As Christians, we're in a constant spiritual battle.**

Where? **On earth as long as we live here**

Why? **The flesh wars against the spirit; the old man fights against the new man**

How? **Through humanistic reasoning and thought processes that claim to be higher than God**

27

You may want to use the PowerPoint slides for this section as you discuss the questions.

As you go through each part of the study for the 2 Corinthians passage, be sure to take the time to explain what you are doing and how it fits into the Inductive Bible Study method.

Since this is the first lesson using the Inductive Bible Study Method, spend extra time going over the five "W" questions, and showing your students how understanding the original language can help us understand the Bible more fully.

DEMOLISHING STRONGHOLDS

Key Words: flesh, carnal, War, weapons, warfare, arguments, thought, God, Christ

CROSS-REFERENCES

Summarize each of the verses and relate them back to 2 Corinthians 10:3–5.

2 Timothy 2:3–4; Ephesians 6:13–18; Colossians 2:8; 2 Corinthians 4:4

What do these verses mean to me?

____

____

How am I going to apply these Scriptures to my life?

____

____

This reference will be assigned for homework for the next lesson. Take the time to get as much as possible from the study of this verse, keeping in mind the context in which it is found.

2 Timothy 2:15

"Be diligent to present yourself approved to God, a worker who does not need to be ashamed, rightly dividing the word of truth."

Who?____________________________________

What?___________________________________

When?___________________________________

Where?__________________________________

Why?____________________________________

28

DEMOLISHING STRONGHOLDS

DEMOLISHING STRONGHOLDS

Key words

Diligent	Approved	Worker	Not ashamed
Dividing	Truth		

CROSS REFERENCES

John 17:17; Psalm 119:160; John 14:6

What is this verse saying to me?

____

____

____

____

How am I going to apply this verse to my life?

____

____

____

____

ADDITIONAL THOUGHTS

____

____

____

____

FIND THE FOCUS

Whenever God gives us new information or repeats something we've heard in the past, He wants us to pay attention. Think for a moment … look back over the notes you have for this lesson, and write down

29

During this part of the lesson each week, it is important to give the teens "alone" time to really meditate on the lesson. If they have the option of spreading out or going to other areas, it might be beneficial to encourage this. Give them a time limit. If at this point in the lesson, you have run out of time, add it to their homework assignment and tell them to fill it in to share next week.

Hand out the "Death and Suffering" article located on the CD-Rom.

See the CD-Rom for the *Optional Activity* for this lesson.

DEMOLISHING STRONGHOLDS

a couple of things that were an encouragement or a challenge, or that stood out to you.

1. ____

____

2. ____

____

HOMEWORK

1. Memorize 2 Timothy 4:4. Practice saying verses 1–4 together.
2. Complete the Inductive Bible Study for 2 Timothy 2:15 from this lesson. Be prepared to discuss your answers.
3. Read through the article on death and suffering before next week's lesson.
4. Pre-read Colossians 2 to prepare your heart for next week's Bible focus.

COUNTERFEIT REALITY

PART 1

IS THIS FOR REAL?

OVERVIEW

Are the teenagers you work with prone to worldly philosophies and practices? If so, these next two sessions will help them to pinpoint areas in their belief system that are not in alignment with a biblical world view.

Bill Jack, a co-founder of World View Academy, an academic, biblical worldview camp for Christian young people, approaches the influence of the media on our culture from another angle, that of how secular worldviews can sway Christians to the point of rationalizing sinful behavior and practices. To further reinforce Bill's lesson, a "Research Project" is assigned for homework. Students are to watch a parent-approved movie and look for the set criterion from the chart provided at the end of the lesson. It's amazing how much more aware of false teaching you become when you are looking specifically for it.

OBJECTIVES

As a result of this lesson, students will be able to:

1. Give several examples of counterfeit reality in our society.
2. Define "secularism."
3. List and explain several attributes of God.
4. Identify the difference between facts and assumptions from movie clips presented.
5. Name the key idea behind scientific evolutionism. *(spiritual blindness)*

BEFORE THE LESSON

Opening Prayer, Announcements, etc.

Review the *Homework*

1. As a group, read the entire memory passage together.
2. Then, have the students divide into small groups of five. Each person in each group gets a turn to recite 2 Timothy 4:1–4, or you could have them do it in pairs to save time. Once completed, the students should form one large group again.
3. Go over the Inductive Bible Study for 2 Timothy 2:15

Object Lesson: "To Tell the Truth"

Materials:

1. Three chairs for the contestants
2. A table with three chairs for the "judges"
3. Three lanyards (yarn is fine) each with a labeled 3x5 card attached, numbered 1 on the first one, 2 on the second one, and 3 on the third one (The contestants will wear a number when they enter for the game)
4. Three pieces of cardstock or stiff paper folded

in half (These will be placed upright as tents revealing the number of the contestant each judge is voting for)

5. Three markers—one each per judge to make notes on his or her cards and to write the number of the contestant he/she is voting for
6. If possible play a show tune (you may be able to purchase for a nominal fee a download of the "What's My Line" theme song to play) for the entrance and exit of the contestants

Procedure:

1. Using an exaggerated announcer's voice, say "Welcome to our (feel free to put the name of your town or church in here) version of *To Tell the Truth*—a well-loved evening game show that ran from the late 1950s through the 1970s. In a moment three contestants will enter and introduce themselves. The object of the game is for the judges to ask questions of the contestants to figure out which individual is the person he/she claims to be. The catch is the judges must ask their questions one after another and will only have five minutes to solve this riddle. Let's give a gracious welcome to our three contestants for *To Tell the Truth.*"
2. (Begin playing show tune music.) Have the three contestants enter with their lanyard numbers on. (Music fades out.) They should remain standing while you read the "job description" and give their introduction.

   Each should introduce themselves as follows:

   "My name is ______ (use the name of the chosen guy and his job), and I am a _____."
2. After their introduction, the contestants may be seated. Say, "Judges, you may begin the questioning now." (Set timer for 5 minutes and begin.)
3. In order, the judges should each ask a question to a particular contestant (e.g., "Contestant #1, how many years have you had this job?). Questions will continue until the timer goes off.
4. Say, "Judges, you must now decide who you think the real _______________ is. Write the number of the contestant on your tent card and be ready to reveal your number when called upon." (Play music while judges vote, then fade out.)
5. Call the first judge's name and say "________, who do you think the real ________ is?" The first judge should respond with "I think the real ______ is Contestant #______" at which time he/she shows the tent card and leaves it standing up on the table in front of him/her.
6. Follow the same procedure with the other two judges.
7. Now announce "Would the real __________ please stand up." More than one of the contestants might show signs of standing up, but the real one will stand all the way up and stay standing. (Applause and surprise from audience really adds to the "reveal.")
8. Say something like "Thank you, contestants, for your willingness to participate in our activity for this lesson." Dismiss them with applause and the game show music playing.

Application:

Whether you realize it or not, the game we just played engaged you in some counterfeit reality. Two of the three people were imposters and tried to convince you that they were something they were not. Every day you face people like that—maybe in real life or through visual media. Do you recognize them? Are you being careful not to fall into the trap of living in their "reality"?

HANDOUT

A key piece in counteracting false teaching is to have a deeper understanding of God's attributes. A condensed chart of these with Scripture references has been included on the CD-Rom. (You may want to consider doing a separate study with your group in the near future on "The Attributes of God" or "The Foundational Doctrines of the Christian Faith" as many young people have never been taught on these issues.)

Have the students turn in their workbooks to Lesson 5 “Laying the Groundwork” in their student workbooks. Instruct them to recite 2 Timothy 4:4 with you. Immediately begin reading the remainder of this section while they follow along.

Make sure all participants have something to write with so that they can actively participate during the DVD presentation.

Following each video presentation, feel free to draw out key points and get feedback from the students. We have built in about 5–7 minutes in this section for such discussion.

COUNTERFEIT REALITY

PART 1

IS THIS FOR REAL?

LAYING THE GROUNDWORK

2 Timothy 4:4 says, “and they will turn their ears away from the truth, and be turned aside to fables.”

The more a person exposes himself to something that does not reflect God’s truth or the light of Christ, i.e., things that are honest, just, pure, lovely, of good report (Philippians 4:8), the easier it is to turn away from the truth and lose interest in knowing it and standing up for it.

This lesson is all about understanding that it’s more than just evolution we have to be aware of and watch out for in our society. Thoughts that emerge from evolution that cause us to rationalize sinful behavior and practices can lead us down a destructive path and keep us from making an impact on our culture.

VIEW THE DVD

(Watch for the key thoughts that complete the statements below and fill them in as you watch and listen.)

Your __worldview__ is your view of the world. . . It is your __framework__ for understanding existence.

We (Christians) are to be __ready__ in season and out of season. The bad news is it’s out of season to preach the __Gospel__. The worse news is it’s __in__ season on Christians.

When you go out and you __proclaim__ the truth of the Gospel, you

31

DEMOLISHING STRONGHOLDS

proclaim that the __Bible__ is true; people are going to come after you. Why?

Because they are immersed in a __counterfeit__ reality. We have a __culture__ that is filled with "myth" information.

Secularism (indifference to or rejection of religion or religious considerations) is a belief that there may or may not be a __God__, but even if there is a God, He's __irrelevant__ in history, art, science, literature, music, philosophy, etc. Secularism is not __neutral__, [it] is a __belief__ system that is __hostile__ and at the core of [it] is the question of __origins__.

Our assumptions determine our __conclusions__.

(As Bill gives the fact or assumption statements below, circle the correct response beside each statement.)

Dimensions of velociraptor	fact	assumption
Half-moon shaped wrist	fact	assumption
"No wonder these things learned how to fly."	fact	assumption
"Perhaps dinosaurs had more in common with modern-day birds than they did with reptiles."	fact	assumption
". . . you spot velociraptor, and you stand still because you think his visual acuity is based on movement just like T-Rex."	fact	assumption

That's __assumption__ on top of assumption on top of __assumption__!

32

Have students turn to Colossians 2 in their Bibles and refer them to the handout from last week, "Original Greek of Key Words."

Call on individuals to each read a verse or two *or* read the chapter to them while they follow along in their Bibles.

Remind them to keep their place in this chapter should they need to refer back to it to answer the questions.

Ask them to put the context of the passage into a sentence. Give them a few minutes in small groups to come up with concise sentences, then join as a large group to go over the items.

DEMOLISHING STRONGHOLDS

"bobbing his head like a bird"	fact	assumption
"Velociraptor is a pack hunter."	fact	assumption

"The attack doesn't come from the front, but from the side."

	fact	assumption

Just because you have _sharp_ *teeth, does that necessarily mean you were designed to eat* _meat_*?*

Six-inch retractable claw	fact	assumption
"slashes at you"	fact	assumption

We are immersed in a counterfeit _**reality**_, and we must realize that people like Dr. Grant are neither stupid, crazy, unintelligent, nor insane. They're _**blind**_.

FYI:

*Science—knowledge; something observable, testable, and repeatable

*Science Fiction—elements of science with a lot of fiction (make believe)

GET INTO THE WORD

Colossians 2:8

"Beware lest anyone cheat you through philosophy and empty deceit, according to the tradition of men, according to the basic principles of the world, and not according to Christ."

Colossians 2 key idea: Don't be led into false teaching or legalism, but follow Christ completely.

Who? ________________________________

What? ________________________________

When? ________________________________

33

DEMOLISHING STRONGHOLDS

DEMOLISHING STRONGHOLDS

Where? ______________________________

Why? ______________________________

How? ______________________________

KEY WORDS

Underline or highlight these words in the verse above.

cheat	philosophy	deceit
tradition	principles	world

CROSS REFERENCES

Acts 17:18; 1 Corinthians 1:30; Colossians 1:16–17; Galatians 4:3, 9–10; 1 John 2:15–17

What is this verse saying to me?

____

____

____

____

How am I going to apply this verse?

____

____

____

____

ADDITIONAL THOUGHTS

____

____

____

____

34

You may want to use the PowerPoint slides for this section as you discuss the questions.

As you go through each part of the study for the Colossians 2 passage, be sure to take the time to explain what you are doing and how it fits into the Inductive Bible Study method.

During this part of the lesson each week, it is important to give the teens "alone" time to really meditate on the lesson. If they have the option of spreading out or going to other areas, it might be beneficial to encourage this. Give them a time limit. If at this point in the lesson, you have run out of time, add it to their homework assignment and tell them to fill it in to share next week.

Hand out the "Research Project" located on the CD-Rom and go over it with your students.

Also give them the "Attributes of God" chart located on the CD-Rom.

There is no *Optional Activity* for Lesson 5.

As mentioned earlier, you may want to consider doing an extra lesson (or a separate study) on the attributes of God.

DEMOLISHING STRONGHOLDS

FIND THE FOCUS

Whenever God gives us new information or repeats something we've heard in the past, He wants us to pay attention. Think for a moment … look back over the notes you have for this lesson, and write down a couple of things that were an encouragement or a challenge, or that stood out to you.

1. ______________________________

2. ______________________________

HOMEWORK

1. Memorize 2 Timothy 4:5. Practice saying verses 1–5 together.
2. Finish any parts of the lesson that were not completed during the lesson time.
3. Complete the Research Project before the next lesson (see below). Be sure to study the "Attributes of God" chart as well.
4. Pre-read 1 Corinthians 8 to prepare your heart for next week's Bible focus.

COUNTERFEIT REALITY PART 2

TIME FOR A REALITY CHECK

By this point in the curriculum, your group has probably shown interest and enthusiasm for the ideas presented. Some or many of them, though, may be feeling that doing something with all this information may be more than they can handle. This is a good place to do a reality check with them. Before beginning the lesson, try to get a feel for how they're feeling about applying what they've learned. Try to set the tone that this is a safe place for them to be open and honest. Work some of their comments into the opening prayer to ask for God's wisdom and strength.

OVERVIEW

The object lesson for this week is a team-building exercise. It is designed to get the teens to think about unity, working together, and being a support to one another. It may be appropriate to build in an additional prayer time after the object lesson to reinforce the concept of being one in Christ.

"See to it that no one takes you captive through philosophy or empty deception according to the tradition of men, according to the elementary principles of the world rather than according to Christ. Don't get captured!" and "People tend to see what they've chosen to believe" are just two of the bold statements Bill shares in this video presentation in this lesson. As he warms up to the crowd, his passion for youth and his concern that they take a stand for Christ so that they don't fall for the world's deception are evident. He challenges the young people to guard their testimonies so that others can see Christ in them.

Note: After this session in the conference, two teenagers accepted Christ as their Savior. What a testimony to the power of God working through his faithful servant.

OBJECTIVES

As a result of this lesson, students will be able to:

1. Explain the difference between science and science fiction.
2. Share an example from the presentation of a movie with a good moral lesson yet steeped in situation ethics.
3. Specify the biblical reasons why UFOs and aliens do not exist.
4. Conclude that evolution kills people.
5. Present the facts/assumptions of one of the clips of a movie shown in this lesson.

BEFORE THE LESSON

Opening Prayer, Announcements, etc.

Review the *Homework*

1. As a group, read the entire memory passage together.
2. Then, have the students divide into small groups of five. Each person in each group gets

a turn to recite 2 Timothy 4:1–5, or you could have them do it in pairs to save time. Once completed, the students should form one large group again.

3. Go over the Inductive Bible Study for 2 Timothy 2:15.
4. Take a few minutes to discuss the results of the "Research Project."

Object Lesson: United We Stand

Materials: ball of yarn; an open area in the meeting room to form a circle

Yarn Circle (excerpted and modified from YouthMinistry.com)

Unity and cooperation are graphically demonstrated in a "yarn circle."

Everyone should stand in a circle. Someone begins by mentioning something he has learned from "Demolishing Strongholds" so far. He then tosses a ball of yarn to another person in the circle, being careful to hang on to the end of the yarn. The recipient of the ball of yarn then mentions something he's learned from this study, and tosses it to another person, holding on to his bit of yarn. This goes on until everyone has had a chance to contribute at least once. By this time, the yarn should have created an intricate pattern, interweaving all of your members.

Then, slowly, a few of the members (every third person in the circle) should drop their sections of yarn, making the pattern sag. In order to take up the slack, all remaining members of the circle must back up. Repeat this a couple of times (every other person dropping out).

Application: It should be brought out that the beautiful pattern was possible only with everyone's involvement. And when some members dropped out of the involvement, the yarn design became ugly and the group was ultimately forced to grow farther apart. Say something like this: "So far in our study, we've covered a lot of material and have delved into some areas that may have made you feel like your contribution to standing for a biblical worldview may not make much difference in this sin-filled world. But let's think of this task as a team effort. I'm sure you've heard the acronym for TEAM—*Together Everyone Achieves More*—and that should be our initial goal with putting into practice what we're learning. God wants to use each and every one of you to make an impact on the culture. He will give you the strength and the opportunities, but you will need to put forth the effort into growing closer to Him and becoming educated so that you can defend the Gospel message. That commission becomes so much more doable when we are working together to learn and to encourage one another."

HANDOUT

The article for this week talks about how a Christian should view aliens and UFOs. Surprisingly, many Christians do not know how to think biblically about this issue. The article is included on the CD-Rom.

Have the students turn in their workbooks to Lesson 6 and in their Bibles to Romans 1:21–22. Call upon individuals to read a portion of the section below.

Make sure all participants have something to write with so that they can actively participate during the DVD presentation.

LESSON

6

COUNTERFEIT REALITY

PART 2

TIME FOR A REALITY CHECK

LAYING THE GROUNDWORK

Read Romans 1:21–22. The Amplified Bible elaborates upon the concept presented in these verses.

> Because when they knew and recognized Him as God, they did not honor and glorify Him as God or give Him thanks. But instead they became futile and godless in their thinking [with vain imaginings, foolish reasoning, and stupid speculations] and their senseless minds were darkened.

In the last lesson, Bill Jack zeroed in on tactics used by humanists to support their theories, i.e., using assumptions and stating them as fact. At the end of the video presentation, Bill made a statement that provided a reasonable explanation for why they (evolutionists) would use counterfeit reality to deceive—they are blind, spiritually blind. They are not saved, and therefore will behave as someone who is influenced by sin and the characteristics of it.

This lesson will continue in the same vein of thought but will also challenge us to use our biblical glasses to be discerning and to be aware of our testimony to those who are not believers or who are new Christians. We have a responsibility to the Lord and to others.

You have been given a lot of information over the past few weeks. Your sense of awareness to the world's influence has been sharpened. Use the tools you've been given to chip away at this counterfeit reality.

37

Demolishing Strongholds

View the DVD

(Watch for the key thoughts that complete the statements below and fill them in as you watch and listen.)

What is the difference between science and science fiction? Science fiction is __**make believe**__ with elements of science. . .science is constrained by __**reality**__.

We who are steeped in a counterfeit reality must tell the world that your best time is after you __**die**__ because you can then get to be with your **Creator**__ forever.

Matthew 11:25

We need to be people of the __**Book**__. We need to be wise in whom we **trust**__. Are we going to trust God's __**Word**__ or man's wisdom?

__**Think**__ your way through [a] film so you are not taken captive by counterfeit reality, but you can use it to start __**conversations**__ with those around you.

Movies are not just entertainment—movies are the most powerful teaching tool in the culture.

38

Following each video presentation, feel free to draw out key points and get feedback from the students. We have built in about 5–7 minutes in this section for such discussion.

Have everyone turn to 1 Corinthians 8 in their Bibles and refer them to the handout from Lesson 4, "Original Greek of Key Words."

Call on individuals to read a verse or two *or* read the chapter to them while they follow along in their Bibles.

Remind them to keep their place in this chapter should they need to refer back to them to answer the questions.

Ask them to put the context of the passage into a sentence. Give them a few minutes in small groups to come up with concise sentences, then join as a large group to go over the items.

You may want to use the PowerPoint slides for this section as you discuss the questions.

DEMOLISHING STRONGHOLDS

Romans 1:25b

This counterfeit reality affects our quest for __meaning__ and significance.

Turn [conversations about movies] into a pulpit from which you can __proclaim__ the truth of the Gospel of Jesus Christ.

"See to it that no one takes you __captive__ through philosophy or empty __deception__ according to the tradition of men ... rather than according to Christ." Don't get __captured__!

The best prison to build is a prison in which the prisoner doesn't even realize he's in prison, because he'll never try to __escape__.

We are all prisoners of our __assumptions__.

If your assumptions are false, it could be __devastating__ . . . __Evolution__ kills people!

BILL'S CONCLUSION

We are steeped in a counterfeit reality, and we have to take what is common to the __culture__ just like Paul did in Acts 17, and we have to turn it into a __pulpit__ from which we proclaim the __truth__ of the Word of God.

GET INTO THE WORD

1 Corinthians 8:1–2

"Now concerning things offered to idols: We know that we all have knowledge. Knowledge puffs up, but love edifies. And if anyone thinks that he knows anything, he knows nothing yet as he ought to know."

1 Corinthians 8 key idea: Though we have freedom in Christ to live as we would like, we need to make sure our behavior does not become a stumbling block to other Christians or to non-Christians.

Who?____

39

DEMOLISHING STRONGHOLDS

DEMOLISHING STRONGHOLDS

What?____________________

When?____________________

Where?____________________

Why?____________________

How?____________________

KEY WORDS

Underline or highlight these words in the verse above.

idols knowledge puffs up edifies knows

What do these verses mean/say?

How can I apply these verses?

ADDITIONAL THOUGHTS

40

As you go through each part of the study for the 1 Corinthians 8 passage, be sure to take the time to explain what you are doing and how it fits into the Inductive Bible Study method.

During this part of the lesson each week, it is important to give the teens "alone" time to really meditate on the lesson. If they have the option of spreading out or going to other areas, it might be beneficial to encourage this. Give them a time limit. If at this point in the lesson, you have run out of time, add it to their homework assignment and tell them to fill it in to share next week.

Hand out the article, "God and the Extraterrestrials" located on the CD-Rom.

Please see the CD-Rom for the *Optional Activity* for this lesson.

DEMOLISHING STRONGHOLDS

FIND THE FOCUS

Think for a moment … look back over the notes you have for this lesson, and write down a couple of things that were an encouragement or a challenge, or that stood out to you.

1. ____

   ____

2. ____

   ____

HOMEWORK

1. Memorize 2 Timothy 4:6. Practice saying verses 1–6 together.
2. Finish any parts of the lesson that were not completed during the lesson time.
3. Read the handout about extraterrestrials before next week. If you have internet access, go to the Answers In Genesis website for further information on this subject (www.answersingenesis.org/go/aliens).
4. Pre-read John 3 and Acts 17 to prepare your heart for next week's Bible focus.

41

DEMOLISHING STRONGHOLDS

ANSWERS TO DIFFICULT ISSUES PART 1

FOSSILS: FACTS OR FICTION?

OVERVIEW

Carl Kerby presents an interesting question in the course of his video presentation for this lesson: Are fossils our friends or foes? By the end of this session, Carl covers the gaps in the fossil record, a biased scientific observation from *Earth Magazine*, and how fossils are formed. He submits to the audience that when we use the Bible as our starting point, the fossil record falls into place with the order of events that Scripture teaches.

Another one of Carl's main thrusts in this session is the responsibility Christians have as missionaries to disseminate the Gospel message. When explaining how fossils are formed, one can convey how such large numbers of these remains could be substantiated by the biblical account of a global catastrophic flood.

The biblical emphasis in this lesson is on accepting the earthly evidence God has provided through His creation and being an example in sharing God's Word. The information piece at the end of this lesson gives an understandable explanation of how fossils are dated by scientists. This in itself is extremely enlightening.

OBJECTIVES

As a result of this lesson, students will be able to:

1. Define "missionary" and how it applies to each of them.
2. Identify what worldviews have to do with fossils.
3. Describe how fossils are formed and how they substantiate the biblical account of a global catastrophic flood.
4. Give at least one example of evidence that refutes the "millions-of-years" theories that evolutionists propagate.

BEFORE THE LESSON

Opening Prayer, Announcements, etc.

Review the *Homework*

1. As a group, read the entire memory passage together.
2. Then, have the students divide into small groups of five. Have them practice reciting 2 Timothy 4:1–6 as a group. Give each group the opportunity to recite the passage for the others. Once completed, the students should form one large group again.
3. Go over any unfinished parts of Lesson 6.
4. Finish any discussion on aliens. (Keep this as brief as possible.)

Object Lesson: Which is oldest?

Materials:

- Several items of different ages, with some things looking older that really aren't
- A table to display them on
- Tape pieces or stickers with numbers to identify each item
- 3x5 cards for the students to write the numbers in order from youngest to oldest

Procedures:

1. Give the students a couple of minutes to examine the numbered objects on the table. (Time them to keep them on track.)
2. Once the time is up, instruct them to write down the order of the items from youngest to oldest.
3. Share the correct order with them.
4. Check by raising hands how many guessed correctly. (Have a treat for those students.)

Application: Say, "Many of you guessed the age based upon appearance and your background knowledge of the items on the table, and many of you guessed wrong. In the same way, many scientists have incorrectly dated fossils and other artifacts because they have the wrong background information. Their presuppositions start with evolution and millions of years. In today's lesson, you will find out how these errors can be made and how to make sure you're viewing fossils with biblical glasses."

HANDOUT

The article for this week is on dating methods—no, not how to get a date, but how scientists determine the dates of rocks and fossils.

After reading this article, students may be eager to discuss its contents. So much of evolution hinges on their claims of "millions of years," and when students realize the dating methods used are unreliable and inconsistent, they may be compelled to "vent" about this deception.

The handout is located on the CD-Rom.

Instruct the students to turn to Lesson 7 "Laying the Groundwork" in their workbooks. Call on individuals to read a portion of this section. Discuss as is appropriate and as time allows.

Make sure all participants have something to write with so that they can actively participate during the DVD presentation.

ANSWERS TO DIFFICULT ISSUES PART 1

FOSSILS: FACT OR FICTION?

LAYING THE GROUNDWORK

2 Timothy 4:5a says, "But you be watchful in all things, endure afflictions." The Greek word for "watchful" in this verse means "to be calm and collected in spirit; to be temperate, dispassionate, and circumspect."

- Temperate: steady, restrained
- Dispassionate: fair, objective
- Circumspect: careful, alert

In other words, Paul's charge to Timothy (and in turn, God's charge to all believers) is to "keep your head" in times of hardship or trouble.

This series of lessons is providing you with many tools to discern truth from myth, increasing your knowledge of the enemy's world system, and equipping you with the Word of God upon which your faith should be founded and solidified. Often, an arsenal such as this can generate a righteous indignation against the evolutionistic/humanistic worldview. When you realize how evolutionists have indoctrinated our schools and culture with false claims, it can stir up your anger. We must guard our hearts to exhibit the self control of a Spirit-filled Christian. The Scriptural command, "Be angry and sin not" means to be angry at the sin, not the sinner. Satan would like nothing better than to discredit our message of truth through a lack of self-restraint when dealing with the opposition. Claim Scripture with confidence: "For God has not given us the spirit of fear; but of power, and of love, and of a *sound mind*" (2 Timothy 1:7).

In lessons 7 and 8, Carl Kerby makes an incredible presentation of the evidence for the biblical account of creation and the Flood through the

42

DEMOLISHING STRONGHOLDS

fossil record. He first reminds us of our great commission to share the good news of the Gospel message. To do this effectively, he challenges us to affirm our faith by always making the Word of God our starting point. When we do this, we have an unshakable foundation upon which to stand and will be able to discern between the scientific facts and evidence we encounter and the fiction of speculations and misleading artwork.

VIEW THE DVD

(Watch for the key thoughts that complete the statements below and fill them in as you watch and listen.)

As a Christian, do you realize that you are a **missionary** of the Gospel of Jesus Christ?

Fossils are one of those areas that many, many difficult **questions** come from.

2 Timothy 4:1–4

What does the world accuse Christians of believing? **Fables**

But the Word of God says that when we start from His Word, we should end up with **truth**.

When you start learning to look at things through the lens of God's **Word** and start learning how to figure out what's **real** and what's not real, you get excited!

John 3:12

Your starting point is going to **influence** the way that you **understand** the world that you live in.

The Word is true—**God** is the only one who's always been there. He told me what happened, and when I **start** with His word, and then I go to the world that I live in, I will understand the world **differently** than somebody who says there is no God. . .

My bias, my axiom, my **presupposition** absolutely **impacts** the way that I understand fossils, stratagraphic layers, light from the furthest star—all of those things!

43

Following each video presentation, feel free to draw out key points and get feedback from the students. We have built in about 5–7 minutes in this section for such discussion.

Have everyone turn to John 3 in their Bibles and refer them to the handout from Lesson 4, "Original Greek of Key Words."

Call on individuals to read a verse or two *or* read the verses to them while they follow along in their Bibles.

Remind them to keep their place in this chapter should they need to refer back to it to answer the questions.

DEMOLISHING STRONGHOLDS

Carl discusses the concept of going through a museum and looking for the evidence that's presented for the evolution side . . .

What you believe about where you come from has a lot to do with how you live your life today.

Is it in the facts? No, it's in the fiction, it's in the __artwork__, the reconstruction.

"Everybody knows fossils are __fickle__. __Bones__ will sing any song you want to hear." That means you can take the same bone, give it to five different people, and they will look at it and come to five different __conclusions__ based upon what their bias or presupposition is.

Watch carefully as Carl covers the gaps in the fossil record, a biased scientific observation from *Earth* Magazine, and how fossils are formed.

If God __judged__ sin the way that He said that He did in the past ... we should find a __record__ of it—and we do.

GET INTO THE WORD

John 3:12

"If I have told you earthly things and you do not believe, how will you believe if I tell you heavenly things?"

44

DEMOLISHING STRONGHOLDS

CONTEXTUAL KEY IDEAS

John 3—Nicodemus, a ruler of the Pharisees, visits Jesus by night to discuss spiritual things. He recognizes that Jesus has been sent from God. Jesus gives Nicodemus a very clear Gospel message and answers his deep questions. In verse twelve, Jesus makes a very relevant connection between believing the earthly things He speaks of, and believing the spiritual truths of the Bible. You can't believe one without the other.

Who?____________________

What?____________________

When?____________________

Where?____________________

Why?____________________

How?____________________

KEY WORDS

tell earthly believe heavenly

What do these verses mean/say?

____

____

____

How can I apply these verses?

____

____

____

Acts 17:11

"These were more fair-minded than those in Thessalonica, in that they received the word with all readiness, and searched the Scriptures daily to find out whether these things were so."

45

Ask an individual to read the context sentences for John 3. (Since both this passage and Acts 17 took a little longer to explain, they were provided for them).

You may want to use the PowerPoint slides for this section.

As you go through each part of the study for the John 3 passage, be sure to take the time to explain what you are doing and how it fits into the Inductive Bible Study method.

Students will complete the Acts 17:11 study as homework for this week.

DEMOLISHING STRONGHOLDS

CONTEXTUAL KEY IDEAS

Acts 17—This chapter encompasses Paul and Silas' visits to Thessalonica and Berea, and then Paul's experiences in Athens, including the speech he gave on Mars Hill. The first half of this chapter clearly emphasizes the importance of deep personal Bible study for believers.

Who?____

What?____

When?____

Where?____

Why?____

How?____

KEY WORDS

Fair-minded	received	readiness	searched
Scriptures	so		

What do these verses mean/say?

____

____

____

How can I apply these verses?

____

____

____

ADDITIONAL THOUGHTS

____

____

____

46

DEMOLISHING STRONGHOLDS

FIND THE FOCUS

Think for a moment … look back over the notes you have for this lesson, and write down a couple of things that were an encouragement or a challenge, or that stood out to you.

1. ______________________________
____
____

2. ______________________________
____
____

HOMEWORK

1. Memorize 2 Timothy 4:7. Practice saying verses 1–7 together.
2. Complete the Inductive Bible Study for Acts 17:11.
3. Read the article about radiometric dating before next week's lesson. Write down any questions or comments you may have in the margins as you are reading.
4. Pre-read Revelation 4 to prepare your heart for next week's Bible focus.

47

During this part of the lesson each week, it is important to give the teens "alone" time to really meditate on the lesson. If they have the option of spreading out or going to other areas, it might be beneficial to encourage this. Give them a time limit. If at this point in the lesson, you have run out of time, add it to their homework assignment and tell them to fill it in to share next week.

Hand out the article, "How Accurate is Fossil Dating?" located on the CD-Rom.

Please see the CD-Rom for the *Optional Activity* for this lesson.

ANSWERS TO DIFFICULT ISSUES PART 2

WHERE'S THE BEEF?

OVERVIEW

In this final video session with Carl Kerby, he gives clear evidence that fossilization does not have to occur over long periods of time as many scientists would lead you to believe. He even shares quotations by two evolutionary scientists that contradict the view evolutionists have of fossil evidence. Doing the work of an evangelist will be highlighted in the introduction of the lesson, and students will also be introduced to a hermeneutic principle (a principle for interpreting Scripture accurately) that will deepen their understanding of Scripture.

OBJECTIVES

As a result of this lesson, students will be able to:

1. Give at least one example of a fossil that contradicts the scientific theory that fossils are made over long periods of time.
2. Identify gaps in the evidence needed to support molecules-to-man evolution.
3. Convey that all of the fossil records show that "turtles have always been turtles, bugs have always been bugs, spiders have always been spiders, etc."
4. Apply the literal interpretation principle of hermeneutics in Bible study.

BEFORE THE LESSON

Opening Prayer, Announcements, etc.

Review the *Homework*

1. As a group, read the entire memory passage together.
2. Then, have the students divide into small groups of five. Have them practice reciting 2 Timothy 4:1–7 as a group. Give each group the opportunity to recite the passage for the others. Once completed, the students should form one large group again.
3. Go over the Inductive Bible Study for Acts 17:11 from Lesson 7.
4. Briefly discuss any questions/concerns about the student's reading of the dating methods used by scientists.

Object Lesson: Science Fakes & Mistakes

An example of how scientists are misguided by their presuppositions is included on the following website: www.bbc.co.uk/sn/prehisoric_life/games/fakes_mistakes/. Intended to be a quiz to point out scientific hoaxes, this activity shows how faulty dating methods and reasoning can illustrate hoaxes of scientific claims of "accurate" information. It would be an extremely effective object lesson for your students.

As you go through each question and answer, be sure to have the students identify the misinformation. Doing such exercises helps to build their confidence when refuting evolution.

Again, in order to use it with a large group, you would need to be able to project the site from a computer to a screen or white wall. If you do not have access to such equipment but have a computer (with internet access) and a printer, you can print the slides from this quiz onto transparencies. Another option would be to print them out and have the teens work in groups to answer one or more questions.

After all the questions have been answered, go over the correct responses, sharing the scientific explanation with each. This is where the object lesson comes into play. The students should be able to pick out facts vs. assumptions, faulty reasoning, and unsubstantiated claims as you go through these. This exercise is a very practical application of Bill Jack's "Counterfeit Reality" sessions.

HANDOUT

The handout for this week is on so-called human evolution. After reading this article, students may be eager to discuss its contents. The evidence and facts your students have been exposed to during this study will have caused them to be much more keen to the deceptions of evolution. You will notice their confidence in defending their faith build as they add more to their "toolbox" each week.

Following the object lesson, have the students turn to Lesson 8, "Laying the Groundwork." Call on individuals to read a portion of this section. Discuss as appropriate and as time allows.

Make sure all participants have something to write with so that they can actively participate during the DVD presentation.

ANSWERS TO DIFFICULT ISSUES PART 2

WHERE'S THE BEEF?

LAYING THE GROUNDWORK

2 Timothy 4:5b boldly states, "Do the work of an evangelist." *Webster's New World Dictionary* defines "evangelist" as "a bringer of good news." Evangelism is defined as a "zealous effort to spread the gospel."

In light of the context of this verse, it is even more vital to share the saving work of Christ at a time such as this when people are not "enduring sound doctrine and are turned unto fables." Are you living your faith? Are you finding opportunities to turn conversations into a pulpit for sharing the evidence of an all-knowing, merciful Creator? Now more than ever Christians need to be proactive in communicating the truth of God's Word.

In this lesson, Carl Kerby continues his focus on fossils and how they provide yet another area of science that confirms the biblical account of Creation. Carl will also show the evidence that refutes the idea that fossilization requires long periods of time.

Following each video presentation, feel free to draw out key points and get feedback from the students. We have built in about 5–7 minutes in this section for such discussion.

VIEW THE DVD

(Watch for the key thoughts that complete the statements below and fill them in as you watch and listen.)

If evolution is true, this is what it should show from the secular quotes:

"__Fossils__ provide the only historical documentary evidence that life has evolved." (** see contradictory statement below.)

48

DEMOLISHING STRONGHOLDS

(Note: As Carl shows the charts displaying the fossil evidence, it will become painstakingly apparent that the fossil record does not provide enough evidence to support evolutionary claims.)

THINK ABOUT IT!

Christian, why are we so willing to sell out the Word of God, the **Rock** that changeth **not**, for something that every time they find a new **stone** somewhere, it **changes** everything we've known for a hundred and fifty years?

What does the **evidence** really show? People have always been **people**; monkeys have always been monkeys …

When you look at the charts, it's almost always the same— **no** evidence where **evolution** is supposed to have happened.

When you start from the Word of God, what we see in the world around us ...
absolutely confirms what we read in the Word of God.

"The gradual change of **fossil species has never been a part of the **evidence** for evolution." No real evolutionist uses the fossil record as evidence in **favor** of the theory of evolution.

They even disagree about what evidence to consider for their side!

The only place you will find evidence for evolution is in the **artwork**.

Carl revisits the question of "Why would a loving God allow death, pain, and suffering? and explains that they (evolutionists) have been blinded to the Gospel because of the "millions-of-years" bias presented by evolution.

When you teach **millions** of years of death and suffering, and that's how we got man, that absolutely **contradicts** what the Word of God

 49

Have the students get into groups of five. Give three 3x5 cards to each group of teens.

Instruct students to turn in their Bibles to each of the references as you come to them.

Call on individuals to read the verses aloud.

Each group should discuss the verses with cross-references. Once a group reaches a consensus about the meaning, a designated "scribe" in the group should write down the meaning. Be sure to tell him or her to label each card with group number and verse reference.

You may want to use the PowerPoint slides for this section.

Allow individuals to write in their personal application for each set of references. Let them share as time allows.

DEMOLISHING STRONGHOLDS

teaches. The Word of God teaches that __man's__ action—sin—led to death and __suffering__.

Fossils—friend or foe? Fossils are our __friends__ when we use the Bible as real history to explain them because … we see that bats have always been bats, cats have always been cats, and that is that. God's __Word__ is __true__ from the beginning.

GET INTO THE WORD

During this lesson's Bible study, we will be applying an inductive method of study based on the "golden rule of interpretation" (refer to lesson 12 for further explanation on biblical hermeneutics—the principles for accurate interpretation of the Scriptures).

The golden rule of interpretation is: "When the plain sense of Scripture makes common sense, seek no other sense." Therefore, take every word at its primary, usual meaning, unless the facts of the immediate context, studied in the light of related passages and fundamental truths, clearly indicate otherwise.

We take the Bible at face value, or plainly, in the same way that we read other literature. This is a common sense approach. We understand that history is history, poetry is poetry, metaphors are metaphors, etc. The Bible is written in many different literary styles and should be read accordingly.

After reading these verses and their cross references and discussing their plain meaning, write down the message you believe God has for you in them.

Revelation 4:11

"You are worthy, O Lord, to receive glory and honor and power; For You created all things, and by Your will they exist and were created."

Cross-reference: Acts 14:15

What do these verses mean/say?

____

____

50 

DEMOLISHING STRONGHOLDS

How can I apply these verses?

____

____

Revelation 10:6

"And swore by Him who lives forever and ever, who created heaven and the things that are in it, the earth and the things that are in it, and the sea and the things that are in it, that there should be delay no longer."

Cross-reference: Jeremiah 10:10

What do these verses mean/say?

____

____

How can I apply these verses?

____

____

Ephesians 6:17

"And take the helmet of salvation, and the sword of the Spirit, which is the word of God:"

Cross-references: Hebrews 4:12: Isaiah 49:2; 1 Peter 1:23

What do these verses mean/say?

____

____

How can I apply these verses?

____

____

During this part of the lesson each week, it is important to give the teens "alone" time to really meditate on the lesson. If they have the option of spreading out or going to other areas, it might be beneficial to encourage this. Give them a time limit. If at this point in the lesson, you have run out of time, add it to their homework assignment and tell them to fill it in to share next week.

Hand out the article, "Only Three Ways to Make an Apeman" located on the CD-Rom.

Please see the CD-Rom for the *Optional Activity* for this lesson.

ADDITIONAL THOUGHTS

____

____

____

FIND THE FOCUS

Think for a moment … look back over the notes you have for this lesson, and write down a couple of things that were an encouragement or a challenge, or that stood out to you.

1. ______________________________________

____

____

2. ______________________________________

____

____

HOMEWORK

1. Memorize 2 Timothy 4:8. Practice saying verses 1–8 together.
2. Finish any parts of Lesson 8 that did not get completed during the lesson time.
3. Read the article "Only Three Ways to Make an Apeman." Write down any questions or comments you may have in the margins as you are reading.
4. Pre-read Colossians 2, Hebrews 9, and 2 Corinthians 10 to prepare your heart for next week's Bible focus.

SIMPLE TOOLS FOR BRAIN SURGERY PART 1

MAY I ASK YOU A QUESTION?

OVERVIEW

The power of a question . . . That's what "Simple Tools for Brain Surgery" is all about. In this session Bill Jack will teach the students a series of four questions that can be used very effectively to cause someone without a biblical worldview to rethink their position. At the end of this lesson, the beliefs of a humanist are shared to help the students better understand the opposition they may face so that they can be more adequately prepared to use the "four questions."

OBJECTIVES

As a result of this lesson, students will be able to:

1. State the four key questions that can be used to make an unsaved person think about his or her foundational beliefs.
2. Identify the biggest problem Christians face in using these questions.
3. Explain why museums are "the secular temples of our day."
4. Specify the goal of this series.
5. Describe the warnings presented in the video regarding the use of the questions.
6. Summarize "Pascal's wager."
7. List several beliefs of a humanist.
8. List the three possibilities that man could claim about what happens after one dies.

BEFORE THE LESSON

Opening Prayer, Announcements, etc.

Review the *Homework*

1. As a group, read the entire memory passage together.
2. Then, have the students divide into small groups of five. Have them practice reciting 2 Timothy 4:1–8 as a group. Give each group the opportunity to recite the passage for the others. Once completed, the students should form one large group again.
3. Go over the unfinished parts from Lesson 8.
4. Briefly discuss any questions/concerns about the student's reading of "Only Three Ways to Make an Apeman."

Object Lesson: Attention-Getters

Materials: One hair dryer and a styling brush; One or two cans of hair spray; Camera for "Before" and "After" photos; Brightly-colored, gawdy clothing; A megaphone or other voice-carrying device; Three small rooms or areas where the different actors can prepare; A bag or more of Smarties™ to provide one per teen

Recruit 4 or 5 teens ahead of time to perform the following tasks:

1. Two or three teens—one to get his/her hair "done" in as crazy a way as possible using hair

spray and a hair dryer, the other one or two to be the stylist(s)

2. One teen to dress in the outlandish clothing
3. One teen to use the megaphone to talk loudly to the crowd

Let the rest of the teens know that you would like them to determine what the three categories have in common when the other students come out. (Be sure to allow for laughing time when you present the recruits.) Tell them they have two minutes to come up with the right answer (use a timer.). The teens will probably blurt out a lot of silly suggestions before getting to the right one. If they are way off in their guesses, you could provide clues. Your goal is to get them to say that all three volunteers are trying to get people's attention or are trying to draw attention to themselves. If they get it correct, give each one a Smartie™. (If they are "rowdy" at this point, wait for them to return to their seats and get settled down.)

Application: There are many ways to get someone's attention. The three we presented today/tonight will accomplish that goal but are not recommended, especially if you want the other person to take you seriously. One very effective way to get and keep someone's attention is by asking questions. In this lesson, Bill Jack will present questions that can be used to engage people in a conversation that will cause them to examine their beliefs more closely and understand that you have an opposing worldview.

HANDOUT

The handout for this week looks at the beliefs of humanists. The information was gathered from a humanist website: www.portlandhumanists.com.

Bill Jack challenges the teens to know their audience and to be prepared for spiritual conversations by trying to learn ahead of time what answers or questions the other side might come up with. One of the first steps in doing this is researching the beliefs of the different worldviews, or belief systems. Since Bill's first "interviewee" in his next session will be a humanist, this information will enable the students to have a better idea of what this man's presuppositions are.

Instruct the students to open their workbooks to Lesson 9. Call on one or two individuals to each read part of "Laying the Groundwork."

Make sure all participants have something to write with so that they can actively participate during the DVD presentation.

Following each video presentation, feel free to draw out key points and get feedback from the students. We have built in about 5–7 minutes in this section for such discussion.

SIMPLE TOOLS FOR BRAIN SURGERY PART 1

MAY I ASK YOU A QUESTION?

LAYING THE GROUNDWORK

In 2 Timothy 4:5c, Paul exhorts Timothy to "fulfill your ministry." The Greek word for "fulfill" is plerophoreo (*play-rof-or-eh'-o*) meaning "to carry out fully (in evidence), i.e., completely assure (or convince), entirely accomplish: most surely believe, fully know (persuade)." Since apologetics is the branch of theology having to do with the defense and proofs of Christianity, it sounds as if this charge encompasses the idea of fully communicating one's faith so that the ministry of reaching the lost for Christ can be realized.

You've been given many ideas in prior lessons as to how you can defend and share your faith. In this lesson, Bill Jack presents another platform that can be used to impact your culture for Christ. In addition, Bill will give you four specific questions that you can learn to use effectively to cause your opponent to think seriously about his/her own beliefs.

VIEW THE DVD

(Watch for the key thoughts that complete the statements below and fill them in as you watch and listen.)

Christians ought not to be ignorant of anything around them.

Four questions that will stand you in good stead no matter what the topic

53

DEMOLISHING STRONGHOLDS

WARNINGS:

1. Christians are to speak the **truth** . . . in **love** . . . by the power of the Holy Spirit.
2. Do **not** use these questions as a **sledge-hammer**, but as one would use a crowbar.

Aristotle said that those who wish to **succeed** must ask the right preliminary—the right beginning—questions.

Sometimes the best you can do is simply get people to think about their own position.

The Four Questions

1. What do you mean by what you're saying?
2. How do you know that what you're saying is true?
3. What difference does what you're saying make in your life? Or So what?
4. What if you are wrong? (or What if you're wrong and you die?)

PASCAL'S WAGER

"If I as a Christian am **wrong** about there being a God, then all I've done is live my life by a set of rules out of a book that has provided nothing but good and **benefit** for mankind, and when I die, that's all there is. But, if you as a non-Christian are wrong about there not being a God and you die, are you willing to **suffer** the consequences?"

What is a humanist?

Humanists

- believe **man** is supreme
- do not believe in God—atheistic
- deny anything **supernatural**

54 

Have the students get into groups of five. Give three 3x5 cards to each group of teens.

Instruct the students to turn in their Bibles to each of the references as you come to them.

Call on individuals to read the verses aloud.

Each group should discuss the verses with cross-references. Once a group reaches a consensus about the meaning, a designated "scribe" in the group should write down the meaning. Be sure to tell him or her to label each card with group number and verse reference.

You may want to use the PowerPoint slides for this section.

Allow individuals to write in their personal application for each set of references. Let them share as time allows.

DEMOLISHING STRONGHOLDS

- believe man is inherently __good__
- believe we can build a civilization by each person deciding for himself what is __right__ and what is __wrong__

Consider the only three answers that could be used to answer, "What happens when you die?"

1. __Nothing__—you die, you rot, you stink, and become extinct
2. __Heaven__ or Hell
3. Reincarnation

GET INTO THE WORD

As you embark on this lesson's study of key verses brought out in Bill's talk, your focus will be once again to interpret these verses at face value. Work in small groups, discuss the context of these verses, and come to a consensus on the meaning. Your leader will guide you through a final discussion to ensure that your interpretation is in line with the intended interpretation for these verses.

Colossians 2:8

"Beware lest anyone cheat you through philosophy and empty deceit, according to the tradition of men, according to the basic principles of the world, and not according to Christ."

Cross References: Jeremiah 29:8; Matthew 15:2–3; Hebrews 13:9

What do these verses mean/say?

____

____

____

DEMOLISHING STRONGHOLDS

How can I apply these verses?

Hebrews 9:27

"And as it is appointed for men to die once, but after this the judgment."

Cross References: Genesis 3:19; Ecclesiastes 3:20

What do these verses mean/say?

How can I apply these verses?

2 Corinthians 10:5

"Casting down arguments and every high thing that exalts itself against the knowledge of God, bringing every thought into captivity to the obedience of Christ;"

Cross References: Isaiah 2:11

What do these verses mean/say?

How can I apply these verses?

56

During this part of the lesson each week, it is important to give the teens "alone" time to really meditate on the lesson. If they have the option of spreading out or going to other areas, it might be beneficial to encourage this. Give them a time limit. If at this point in the lesson, you have run out of time, add it to their homework assignment and tell them to fill it in to share next week.

Hand out the article, "General Humanist Beliefs" located on the CD-Rom.

Please see the CD-Rom for the *Optional Activity* for this lesson.

DEMOLISHING STRONGHOLDS

ADDITIONAL THOUGHTS

____

____

____

FIND THE FOCUS

Think for a moment ... look back over the notes you have for this lesson, and write down a couple of things that were an encouragement or a challenge, or that stood out to you.

1. ____

   ____

   ____

2. ____

   ____

   ____

HOMEWORK

1. Review 2 Timothy 4:1–8.
2. Finish any parts of the lesson that did not get completed during the lesson time.
3. Read the article "General Humanist Beliefs" in preparation for next week's DVD presentation.
4. Pre-read Romans 1 to prepare your heart for next week's Bible focus.

57

SIMPLE TOOLS FOR BRAIN SURGERY PART 2

THE UNCUT VERSION

OVERVIEW

Today's lesson centers on the concept of sowing seeds in the hearts of those who reject a biblical worldview. It is important that as you disciple the teens in your care, you reinforce to them that they may never be able lead an evolutionist to the Lord—that's not the job God has called us to. Our job is to share our faith and His Word—He will bring the increase. If all we are able to do is to cause the opposition to begin to question their beliefs, we have accomplished much. Bill Jack gives two practical illustrations of how one can do just that. He also shares about an ongoing friendship he has developed with the evolutionist in his video—the man has not received Christ, but he continues to ask questions. Indeed, Bill's use of the "four questions" has exemplified that of a crowbar rather than a sledgehammer.

OBJECTIVES

As a result of this lesson, students will be able to:

1. Identify flaws in the belief system of the individuals interviewed on the video.
2. Give at least one example of a situation in which a historical person made a choice that was not for the good of mankind.
3. Tell about at least one instance that an evolutionist will show a belief in absolutes.

BEFORE THE LESSON

Opening Prayer, Announcements, etc.

Review the *Homework*

1. As a group, recite the entire memory passage together.
2. Go over the unfinished parts from Lesson 9.
3. Allow those students who researched atheism and the New Age Movement to share some of the beliefs of these religions.

Object Lesson: A Problem with the Foundation

Materials: Fine sand (available in hobby stores); Squirt guns (preferably enough for each student to use one—these are usually available at stores such as dollar stores, Wal-Mart, or Target; Water source to fill the squirt guns prior to the meeting; A small unbreakable bowl; A pan in which to place the sand and bowl

Before the lesson, gather enough sand to make a small, pointed pile. Set a small, unbreakable bowl on top of it. After opening prayer and announcements, pass out the squirt guns so that each student has one. Call on one student to try to squirt enough water into the sand under the bowl that the bowl slides off. Time him/her for 30 seconds. Have two more students join the first student with the same mission. Finally, have everyone form a tight circle. When you say "Go," they should all begin squirting the sand. Let them continue until the bowl has tipped and lost its support.

Application: When just one of you or even three of you tried to squirt enough water to loosen the sand, it was a big job. Yet, when all of you used your "ammunition," it didn't take long at all to loosen the sand and cause the bowl to tip off its "foundation." Likewise, the influence of Christ in our society can be so much more powerful (and able to weaken the evolutionary foundation of the culture) if *all* of us are living, talking, and promoting the biblical worldview together.

HANDOUT

This week the handout teaches your students that we must not leave our biblical presuppositions out of our discussions with skeptics, because our entire worldview is based on the truth of God's Word. The article, "Debate Terms" is located on the CD-Rom.

Instruct the students to open their workbooks to Lesson 10. Call on one or two individuals to each read part of "Laying the Groundwork."

Make sure all participants have something to write with so that they can actively participate during the DVD presentation.

SIMPLE TOOLS FOR BRAIN SURGERY PART 2

THE UNCUT VERSION

LAYING THE GROUNDWORK

In 2 Timothy 4:6–7a, the Apostle Paul writes,

> "For I am already being poured out as a drink offering, and the time of my departure is at hand. I have fought the good fight . . ."

Wow! What an incredible testimony! Paul knows that he has done God's will and served Him faithfully. He knows he is close to death, and he is ready to meet his Lord. This is a peace that passes all understanding. Though he still refers to his Christian walk as a "fight," he is completely at peace because he is confident that he has fulfilled God's purpose for his life and is now ready to "be present with the Lord" (2 Corinthians 5:8). When a Christian walks according to God's will and actively lives and shares his faith, he too can have the confidence conveyed here by Paul.

In this session, Bill Jack will be interviewing a humanist and an atheist. As you observe, you will hear some philosophies that have no basis in truth, or evidence to support them. Try to view these individuals through the eyes of Jesus, i.e., see them as lost and in need of Christ, and notice how blinded they are by their false religion.

At the end of this lesson, you will find some very sound advice from Ken Ham, President of Answers in Genesis, on how to effectively talk to an evolutionist using the Bible as your starting point.

58

VIEW THE DVD

(Watch for the key thoughts that complete the statements below and fill them in as you watch and listen.)

During this video, write down some of the words/phrases used by the humanist and the evolutionists at the "Freedom from Religion" booth at the People's Fair in downtown Denver.

Humanist Ideas:

Too often not only are we soft-headed, but we are hard-hearted ... We ought to be thinking God's thoughts after Him. We ought to be the most tender-hearted towards people.

Evolutionist Ideas:

59

Following each video presentation, feel free to draw out key points and get feedback from the students. We have built in about 5–7 minutes in this section for such discussion.

Instruct students to turn to Romans 1 in their Bibles.

Call on individuals to each read a verse or two until the chapter has been read.

Each group should discuss the verses with cross-references. Once a group reaches a consensus about the meaning, a designated "scribe" in the group should write down the meaning. Be sure to tell him or her to label each card with group number and topic.

You may want to use the PowerPoint slides for this section.

Isaiah 55:11 will be given for homework for this week.

DEMOLISHING STRONGHOLDS

____

____

____

____

____

GET INTO THE WORD

Write down and reference key phrases from **Romans 1** that refer to creation, evolution, and consequences. God is very clear in these verses, and it's important that you understand the cause and effect present in this key passage of Scripture.

Creation _______________________________________

____

____

Evolution _______________________________________

____

____

Consequences ____________________________________

____

____

Isaiah 55:11

"So shall My word be that goes forth from My mouth; it shall not return to Me void, but it shall accomplish what I please, and it shall prosper in the thing for which I sent it."

Cross reference: Isaiah 46:10

60

DEMOLISHING STRONGHOLDS

What do these verses mean/say?

____

____

How can I apply these verses?

____

____

____

FIND THE FOCUS

Think for a moment … look back over the notes you have for this lesson, and write down a couple of things that were an encouragement or a challenge, or that stood out to you.

1. ______________________________________
   ____
2. ______________________________________
   ____

HOMEWORK

1. Review 2 Timothy 4:1–8.
2. Complete the Inductive Bible Study for Isaiah 55:11.
3. Read the article "Debate Terms."
4. Pre-read Revelation 5 and Colossians 3 to prepare your heart for next week's Bible focus.

61

During this part of the lesson each week, it is important to give the teens "alone" time to really meditate on the lesson. If they have the option of spreading out or going to other areas, it might be beneficial to encourage this. Give them a time limit. If at this point in the lesson, you have run out of time, add it to their homework assignment and tell them to fill it in to share next week.

Hand out the article, "Debate Terms" found on the CD-Rom.

Please see the CD-Rom for the *Optional Activity* for this lesson. You may want to work through the Gospel presentation part with any students who may lack confidence.

SPECIAL FORCES FOR THE SAVIOR PART 1

A MINORITY REPORT

OVERVIEW

Today's lesson is the first of two sessions by Dr. Charles Ware, President of Crossroads Bible College in Indianapolis, IN. Throughout his talk, Dr. Ware shares stories of prejudice and discrimination that he and others have endured because of their skin color to show a relationship to the persecution that may be experienced by those who are committed to being part of God's "special forces." Though this is an issue not commonly dealt with in churches, Dr. Ware presents the material in an appropriate and heartfelt manner.

OBJECTIVES

As a result of this lesson, students will be able to:

1. Diagnose the cause of racial problems in our society.
2. Prioritize the concepts presented in Revelation 5.
3. Compare/contrast Christians as minorities with the rest of culture.
4. Examine themselves in relation to bias/prejudice in their lives compared to biblical principles.

BEFORE THE LESSON

Opening Prayer, Announcements, etc.

Review the *Homework*

1. As a group, recite the entire memory passage together.
2. Go over the Inductive Bible Study for Isaiah 55:11 from Lesson 10.
3. Give several students the opportunity to share their testimonies (Optional Activity). Allow them to read from their paper if that's more comfortable for them.
4. Briefly discuss the information about "Debate Terms" from their homework reading.

Object Lesson: Talk Sparkers

Use this portion of the lesson to get the students thinking about today's subject. Begin by using these Scriptures to enrich your discussions about social issues: Matthew 25:31–46; Luke 10:25–37; Galatians 3:26–29.

Talk-Sparkers About Social Issues

- Describe a time when you felt like a victim of racial, social, or religious prejudice. What's a Christian's responsibility in these situations?
- Agree or disagree: "Minorities in America deserve preferred treatment today because of the mistreatment they received in the past."

HANDOUT

This week's handout looks at the issue of "race" from a biblical perspective and shows your students that all humans are "of one blood."

SPECIAL FORCES FOR THE SAVIOR PART 1

A MINORITY REPORT

LAYING THE GROUNDWORK

"I have finished the race, I have kept the faith" (2 Timothy 4:7b).

In spite of opposition, persecution, prison, beatings, shipwreck, weariness, hunger and thirst, cold, and numerous other perils (2 Corinthians 11:23–27), Paul endured as a servant and soldier of the Lord. His faith never wavered. Why is that?

If you have never read all of Paul's epistles, let this be a challenge to you to do so. Not only will you discover why he was so committed to Christ, you'll also learn foundational Christian doctrine that is vital for all believers. Paul was consistent in his witness because his starting point was ***always*** God's Word. He knew a joy and peace only God can give because he had a heart of gratitude for what the Lord had done for him. Paul's example to us is to know the Bible and know the God of the Bible.

You are about to see and hear Dr. Charles Ware who uses this inspiring session to get us to acknowledge what an awesome God we have. He also calls us to stand firm in our faith as a Christian minority. We are called out to stand up for Jesus, and we are to be prepared for the opposition we face. We must be ready to answer their questions and accusations.

TERM TO DEFINE:

Jim Crow laws—*Jim Crow laws* were state and local laws enacted in the Southern and border states of the United States and in force between 1876 and 1964 that restricted access of African-Americans to public facilities. *Jim Crow*, or the *Jim Crow period* or the *Jim Crow era* refers to the time during which this practice occurred. The most important laws required that public schools be segregated

62

Instruct the students to open their workbooks to Lesson 11. Call on one or two individuals to each read part of "Laying the Groundwork."

Make sure all participants have something to write with so that they can actively participate during the DVD presentation.

Following each video presentation, feel free to draw out key points and get feedback from the students. We have built in about 5–7 minutes in this section for such discussion.

by race, and that most public places (including trains and buses) have separate facilities for whites and blacks. School segregation was declared unconstitutional by the Supreme Court in 1954 in Brown v. Board of Education. All the other Jim Crow laws were repealed by the Civil Rights Act of 1964.

VIEW THE DVD

(Watch for the key thoughts that complete the statements below and fill them in as you watch and listen.)

Revelation 5

You need to understand that you're partnering with a God who ultimately __wins__ this battle, and you'll go on to be amongst those thousands of thousands, ten thousand times ten thousand as we worship Him who alone is __worthy__!

__Special__ Forces are not majorities, they are __minorities__.

Dr. Ware wants to "challenge you to dream a bit, to __dream__ about what a sovereign all-powerful God can do through a minority, what he can do through one person like you."

Listen carefully as Dr. Ware gives deep insight into understanding the cultural differences we may encounter in America.

In the Scriptures, the __people__ of God were a called-out group. Those who come to faith in Christ __repent__ of their sins and come to faith in Christ. They are brought together as one in Christ. We are the __family__ of God. We stand against a society . . . that has a culture and a worldview that __denies__

The problem is not skin, it's sin.
Jesus Christ wants us to come together across racial and economic lines for the glory of God!

63

DEMOLISHING STRONGHOLDS

our God and denies the **authority** of His Word. We're not to be **separated**, but we're to be unified on biblical **truth**.

Do you know that one of the strongholds of your society is that they're continually attacking Christianity based upon bigotry and **prejudice**?

Expect **challenges**. . . 2 Timothy 2: "Endure hardness as a good soldier."

DISCUSSION/THOUGHT QUESTIONS:

1. Maybe the only cultural difference of which you could be a victim has to do with your Christian worldview versus the anti-Christian worldviews. Are you prepared to stand alone or be a leader in this minority? If not, what's holding you back?
2. Less than 6% of Protestant churches are what we can call multiethnic or multicultural. Why do you think that is? Examine yourself. Are you biased or prejudiced?

GET INTO THE WORD

Each of the passages for today's lesson has a different thrust. The first one is focusing on the person and work of Jesus Christ. Answer the following questions after reading the passage to gain a deeper understanding of the context of this passage as you apply the contextual principle of hermeneutics.

Revelation 5:6–14

The apostle John describes Jesus as what animal? **A Lamb**

Why? **Jesus is the perfect Lamb of God who was slain to pay for the sins of the world.**

What is the purpose of the book of Revelation? **To show his servants things which must shortly come to pass (Rev. 1:1).**

things which must shortly come to pass (Rev. 1:1).

64

Instruct students to turn to Revelation 5, and then Colossians 3 in their Bibles.

Call on individuals to read a verse or two until the passage has been read. Follow this procedure for both passages.

Ask the questions and call on students to give the answers.

You may want to use the PowerPoint slides for this section.

Give them quiet time to write in their applications for these passages.

DEMOLISHING STRONGHOLDS

Jesus is called "worthy" to receive what seven blessings from His people?

Power, riches, wisdom, strength, honor, glory, and blessing

The events of the book of Revelation will usher in the restoration of all things to God's created perfection and the consummation of all His purposes in creation. What an all-wise God we have, and what a wonderful future we have to look forward to!

How can I apply these verses?

___

___

___

___

The second passage reminds us of who we are in Christ and how we are to exemplify the "new man" within us.

Colossians 3:10–15

v. 10 Whose image are all believers created in? the image of God

v. 11 What point is Paul trying to get across here? Who is to be the center of our thoughts?

Christ is to be everything to us; we are not to be caught up in giving preferential treatment to anyone but Him. If Christ is preeminent in our lives, then we will be able to get along with others for His glory.

vv. 12–14 List and explain in your own words the godly character traits we are commanded to attain. After your leader gives deeper insight into these traits and their biblical significance, be sure to add to your notes. What you see, hear, say, and do will remain in your memory much longer than if you are only listening.

Tender mercies—"bowels of mercies" (KJV). The Hebrews regarded the bowels as the seat of the tenderer affections, esp. kindness, benevolence, compassion; hence our heart

65

DEMOLISHING STRONGHOLDS

(tender mercies, affections, etc.); a heart in which mercy resides

Kindness—moral goodness, integrity

Humility—having a humble opinion of one's self; a deep sense of one's (moral) littleness; modesty, humility, lowliness of mind

Meekness—gentleness, mildness

Longsuffering—patience, endurance, constancy, steadfastness, perseverance; slowness in avenging wrongs

Forgiveness—to do something pleasant or agreeable (to one), to do a favor to, gratify; to show one's self gracious, kind, benevolent; to pardon; to give graciously, give freely, bestow; graciously to restore one to another; to preserve for one a person in peril

Love—brotherly love, affection, goodwill, benevolence

How can I apply these verses?

ADDITIONAL THOUGHTS

66

During this part of the lesson each week, it is important to give the teens "alone" time to really meditate on the lesson. If they have the option of spreading out or going to other areas, it might be beneficial to encourage this. Give them a time limit. If at this point in the lesson, you have run out of time, add it to their homework assignment and tell them to fill it in to share next week.

Hand out the article, "Is there Really Just One Race?" located on the CD-Rom.

There is no *Optional Activity* for Lesson 11.

DEMOLISHING STRONGHOLDS

FIND THE FOCUS

Think for a moment … look back over the notes you have for this lesson, and write down a couple of things that were an encouragement or a challenge, or that stood out to you.

1. ______________________________

____

____

2. ______________________________

____

____

HOMEWORK

1. Review 2 Timothy 4:1–8.
2. Finish any parts of the lesson that did not get completed during the lesson time.
3. Read the article "Is There Really Just One Race?"
4. Read Romans 1 again to prepare your heart for next week's Bible focus.

67

SPECIAL FORCES FOR THE SAVIOR PART 2

THE "DREAM" TEAM

OVERVIEW

In a continuation of Dr. Charles Ware's delivery of "Special Forces for the Savior," he creates an enthusiasm for the message through effective illustrations and key Scripture passages. He challenges the teenagers to "learn the Book" that they might be able to stand firm against the forces of this world. The chief aim of this lesson is to provoke the teens to make a commitment to becoming students of the Word.

OBJECTIVES

As a result of this lesson, students will be able to:

1. Give examples of Christians who have fallen into sin, repented, and experienced forgiveness and usefulness to God afterward.
2. Relate some of the hard choices they have had to make or will have to make to stand up for their faith.
3. Use the proper hermeneutical principles to interpret the Scriptures.
4. Identify the original vs. the culturally accepted definitions of "tolerance."
5. State/explain what is the greatest evangelistic marketing tool a Christian has.

BEFORE THE LESSON

Opening Prayer, Announcements, etc.

Review the *Homework*

1. As a group, recite the entire memory passage together.
2. Go over the unfinished parts from Lesson 11.
3. Take a few minutes to discuss the "One Race" article from Lesson 11.

Object Lesson: Get a Clue

We've been learning a lot in this study about properly understanding and applying God's Word. One of the concepts that has been communicated to you is that of cross-referencing and comparing Scripture with Scripture. Let's do a *Sword Drill* for fun and see if we can apply some of this knowledge.

Matthew 4:19 Matthew 10:22

Matthew 27:5 Luke 10:37b

If we were to connect the message of these individual verses to try to gain some meaning, we'd have a very discouraging and inaccurate interpretation. Yet many people will read random passages without delving into the context of each passage and claim they "don't get anything" out of the Bible. Just as a driver's manual must be learned before you can knowledgeably navigate a car, so God's Word must be read, studied, and meditated upon for you to successfully navigate your Christian walk.

HANDOUT

The handout on Bible interpretation for this week will give your students several principles they can use in their own personal Bible study. This is located on the CD-Rom.

SPECIAL FORCES FOR THE SAVIOR PART 2

THE "DREAM" TEAM

Instruct the students to turn in their workbooks to Lesson 12. Call on individuals to read a portion of this section while the others follow along.

Make sure all participants have something to write with so that they can actively participate during the DVD presentation.

LAYING THE GROUNDWORK

Today, we will first take a closer look at 2 Timothy 4:8, the final verse in our memory passage. By itself, it could lead one to believe that all believers might be entitled to a "crown of righteousness" when we stand before the Lord; however, within the context of the passage and the Apostle Paul's life, it is apparent that this special reward is presented to those who have stayed faithful and committed to serving the Lord, and as a result, "love his appearing."

What an encouragement it is to read 2 Timothy 4:8, the final verse in our memory passage:

> Finally, there is laid up for me the crown of righteousness, which the Lord, the righteous Judge, will give to me on that Day, and not to me only but also to all who have loved His appearing.

Dr. Joe Temple, Bible teacher for over 50 years, in his sermon series on "The Five Crowns" makes the following observation: "Every man who loves the appearing of the Lord will receive the crown, because you cannot love His appearing without fighting a good fight. You cannot love His appearing without running a good race. You cannot love His appearing without guarding the faith."

Because as Christians we believe that this life is simply preparation for eternity, we have a goal and a hope. Our work is not in vain (1 Corinthians 15:58) and it *shall* be rewarded (2 Chronicles 15:7; 1 Corinthians 3:10–15) by the King of Kings and Lord of Lords. Even when we fall,

68 

DEMOLISHING STRONGHOLDS

and we *will* fall, we can come to God's throne of grace, confess, receive restored fellowship with our Lord (1 John 1:9), and carry on His work with renewed wisdom and experience (James 1:2–5).

In this second session of "Special Forces for the Savior," Dr. Ware reiterates the concept that Christian people make mistakes and fail because we live in a sinful, fallen world. He states that, "God has revealed in His Word that some of the people He has used in His mercy and His grace to accomplish His will have been people of clay feet. They have fallen. God has (through their experiences) shown me . . . the pattern that I need to follow." Dr. Ware then uses the acronym DREAM to show us the pattern God has established for those whom He has called to demolish the strongholds of the world's belief system.

Following each video presentation, feel free to draw out key points and get feedback from the students. We have built in about 5–7 minutes in this section for such discussion.

VIEW THE DVD

(There are no notes to fill in for this session, but students may want to jot down some thoughts during the DVD.)

Understand (that) just because one (or more) of God's people fell, it doesn't mean that __**God**__ is unfaithful. God has been working His __**will**__, in His __**mercy**__ and His grace, through ordinary fallen sinners for years, and still is!

____

____

____

____

____

____

____

____

____

____

DEMOLISHING STRONGHOLDS

Will you have a biblical worldview that you can both "lip" and live in such a way that others will be convinced you're for real—you're genuine?

GROUP DISCUSSION

1. Part of the application is studying for yourself, getting to know the subject that you will be defending. Become a Berean and search the Scriptures for yourself (Acts 17:11). Discuss what areas would be good for an in-depth personal study.
2. Discuss the difference between the original definition of tolerance (to respect others as people while not agreeing with their beliefs/ practices) and the current cultural definition (to condone or agree with others' beliefs/practices without sharing them).
3. Dr. Ware states that the greatest marketing tool for Christianity is the love we have for one another. Discuss with the group what you believe this conveys.
4. Are you prepared to defend your faith from God's Word? Are you ready to commit to the authority of God's Word?
5. What did Dr. Ware mean by: "God doesn't have fans. We are all players"?

GET INTO THE WORD

In this lesson, we are going to apply some of the hermeneutic principles to Romans 1, the chapter we looked at in Lesson 10. Our focus will be Principle #3: The Scripture interprets Scripture Principle. Listed below are cross-references to most of the verses in this chapter. You will work in small groups to share the responsibility of looking up the verses and

70

Discuss the questions here as a group.

Hand out the article, "The Principles of Biblical Interpretation" located on the CD-Rom. You may use the PowerPoint slides to go over each principle. Be sure to highlight Principle #3 since they will be applying that on in this lesson.

Instruct everyone to turn to Romans 1 in his or her Bible.

Call on individuals to each read a verse or section until the passage has been read.

Divide the students into groups of 3 or 4 and allow them to work through this section.

Give them any unfinished part as homework.

DEMOLISHING STRONGHOLDS

comparing them with the corresponding verse from Romans 1. Do as many as you have time for and try to get to the rest of them throughout the next week.

1:2 (cf. Luke 1:70; Titus 1:2) ____________________

____

1:4 (cf. Hebrews 9:13–15) ____________________

____

1:5 (cf. Ephesians 3:8–9)____________________

____

1:9 (cf. Ephesians 1:16; Philippians 1:3; 1 Thessalonians 1:2)

____

____

1:13 (cf. Romans 15:22; 1 Thessalonians 2:18)

____

____

1:16 (cf. Acts 3:26; 1 Corinthians 1:18)

____

____

1:17 (cf. Habakkuk 2:4; Galatians 3:11)

____

____

1:19 (cf. John 1:9; Acts 14:17)____________________

____

1:20 (cf. Psalm 19:1)____________________

____

71

DEMOLISHING STRONGHOLDS

1:21 (cf. 2 Kings 17:15; Ephesians 4:17)

1:22 (cf. Jeremiah 10:14; 1 Corinthians 1:20)

1:23 (cf. Psalm 106:20; Jeremiah 2:11)

1:24 (cf. Psalm 81:12; 1 Peter 4:3)

1:26 (cf. 1 Thessalonians 4:5) ______

1:27 (cf. Leviticus 18:22; Leviticus 20:13; 1 Corinthians 6:9)

1:28 (cf. Ephesians 5:4) ______

1:30 (cf. 2 Timothy 3:2) ______

1:31 (cf. 2 Timothy 3:3) ______

1:32 (cf. Romans 6:21, 23) ______

72

During this part of the lesson each week, it is important to give the teens "alone" time to really meditate on the lesson. If they have the option of spreading out or going to other areas, it might be beneficial to encourage this. Give them a time limit. If at this point in the lesson, you have run out of time, add it to their homework assignment and tell them to fill it in to share next week.

Challenge your students to apply one or more of the principles from the handout to their daily Bible reading.

There is no *Optional Activity* for this lesson.

DEMOLISHING STRONGHOLDS

What is the overall message of Romans 1 in light of the comparable Scripture?____________________

____

How can I apply these verses?

____

____

FIND THE FOCUS

Think for a moment … look back over the notes you have for this lesson, and write down a couple of things that were an encouragement or a challenge, or that stood out to you.

1. ____________________

2. ____________________

HOMEWORK

1. Review 2 Timothy 4:1–8.
2. Finish any parts of the lesson that did not get completed during the lesson time.
3. Read the article about biblical hermeneutics—the principles of accurate interpretation of the Bible.
4. Write down one or two things you've learned from God's Word and be prepared to share when you come to the final class for Lesson 13.

73

Q&A SESSION

OVERVIEW

In this final session, Bill Jack goes on the streets to talk with college students about their beliefs and to challenge them with "The Four Questions." This session will help teens understand more how non-Christians think, and they will be able to see Bill use good questioning techniques to reveal the inconsistencies in their worldviews.

OBJECTIVES

As a result of completing this lesson, students will be able to:

1. Utilize the answers provided to questions in this session to help them present a biblical worldview.
2. Quote 2 Timothy 4:1–8 from memory.
3. Construct a list of situations in which they could turn a conversation into a Gospel presentation.

BEFORE THE LESSON

Opening Prayer, Announcements, etc.

Review the *Homework*

1. As a group, recite the entire memory passage together.
2. Go over the unfinished parts from Lesson 12.
3. Discuss any questions they may have from the handout on biblical interpretation.

Note: Instead of an object lesson today, use this time to pass out paper or 3x5 cards and have everyone write down one or two things that he or she gleaned from God's Word over the past week. Let several students share as time permits.

LESSON

13 Q&A SESSION

LAYING THE GROUNDWORK

The Christian life can be a real battleground! Throughout his epistles, Paul uses military terminology to emphasize the Christian's role and goes as far as to relate our spiritual "equipment" to that of earthly armor and weapons (Ephesians 6:10–18).

Paul's first letter to Timothy is filled with encouragement for a young Christian man who was facing many difficult problems in his place of service for the Lord.

> "One of the key words in 1 Timothy is 'charge,' sometimes translated 'commandment' (1:3, 5, 18; 4:11; 5:7; 6:13, 17). It was a military term, referring to an order to be passed down the line. God had entrusted the Gospel to Paul (1:11), who had passed it along to Timothy (1:18–19; 6:20). Timothy was 'charged' to guard this treasure (2 Timothy 1:13–14) and pass it along to faithful people who would, in turn, entrust it to others (2 Timothy 2:2)."
>
> —*Weirsbe's Expository Outlines*, p. 619.

1 Timothy 4:16 is one of those charges given to Timothy:

> "Take heed to yourself and to the doctrine. Continue in them, for in doing this you will save both yourself and those who hear you."

Just like you, Timothy lived in a day and age where false teaching, worldly philosophies, and heresies permeated his culture.

Have the students turn to Lesson 13 in their workbooks. Call on individuals to each read a portion of this section.

Make sure all participants have something to write with so that they can actively participate during the DVD presentation.

DEMOLISHING STRONGHOLDS

In this verse, Paul emphasizes the necessity of first *examining yourself* to find out where you are spiritually and where you are going.

Next, he focuses in on *examining your doctrines* to make sure they are in line with God's Word.

Finally, the challenge shifts from examination to *application—continue, remain faithful, persevere in your faith and the teachings of God's Word.*

Why? It's about salvation—yours and others'. In Christ alone is eternal security, love, joy, and peace.

VIEW THE DVD

To culminate our study of what it takes to demolish strongholds, we will watch Bill Jack as he does some man-on-the-street interviews and demonstrates how one might use the "The Four Questions." Below are lines for you to take notes. Be sure to jot down any questions or comments that you find helpful or interesting. Remember, it is through the work of God's Word that He can break down the barriers and demolish the strongholds of opposing worldviews.

75

DEMOLISHING STRONGHOLDS

GET INTO THE WORD

Look back over the previous lessons and pick two or three verses that have really challenged your faith through this study. Discuss them with the group and use your discussion as a springboard to share how this series of lessons has made a difference in your walk with and service for God.

What verses have really spoken to you throughout the *Demolishing Strongholds* course?

How will you apply or how have you already applied what you've learned?

76

Give the teens several minutes to look over their lessons for meaningful verses and to record what they have learned and how they might apply it in their lives.

DEMOLISHING STRONGHOLDS

FIND THE FOCUS

Think for a moment … look back over the notes you have for this lesson, and write down a couple of things that were an encouragement or a challenge, or that stood out to you.

1. ____

   ____

2. ____

   ____

A FINAL WORD

Now you can say with Paul, "I have finished my course," though this "course" was quite insignificant compared to Paul's journey through life. The challenge to you now is to stay faithful and to use what you have learned. You now have several important tools with which to arm yourself.

1. Your sword, God's Word, is your offensive weapon against the opposition you will face in life. Read it, learn from it, and apply it.
2. The information you have gleaned from this course has better equipped you to defend your faith, counter the skeptics, and challenge nonbiblical worldviews.
3. Use the Answers in Genesis website where you will find over 5,000 free articles with faith-building content to engage and equip you.

Matthew 25:21

His lord said to him,
"Well done, good and faithful servant;
you were faithful over a few things,
I will make you ruler over many things.
Enter into the joy of your lord."

77